Hearing *the* Master's Voice

Hearing *the* Master's Voice

The Comfort and Confidence of Knowing God's Will

Robert Jeffress

WaterBrook Press

HEARING THE MASTER'S VOICE
PUBLISHED BY WATERBROOK PRESS
2375 Telstar, Suite 160
Colorado Springs, Colorado 80920
A division of Random House, Inc.

ISBN 1-57856-248-1

Published in association with Sealy M. Yates, Literary Agent, Orange, California.

Library of Congress Cataloging-in-Publication Data
Jeffress, Robert, 1955–
Hearing the Master's voice : the comfort and confidence of knowing God's will / Robert Jeffress.—1st ed.
p. cm.
ISBN 1-57856-248-1
1. Christian life. 2. God—Will. I. Title.

BV4501.2 .J394 2001
248.4—dc21

00-067316

Printed in the United States of America
2001—First Edition

10 9 8 7 6 5 4 3 2 1

To Stanley and Jodie Williamson

and

John and Janice Hyatt

---

for your vision and support for
our Pathway to Victory television ministry.
Thank you for your obedience
to the Master's voice.

Contents

Acknowledgments ix

Part One: Understanding the Master's Voice

1. Where There's God's Will, There Must Be a Way 1
   Three common approaches to discovering God's will...
   and why they don't work

2. Scrutinizing the Inscrutable 19
   What you can *know and what you will* never *know*
   about God's will for your life

Part Two: Hearing the Master's Voice

3. The Bible Tells Me So? 41
   "If the Bible is so wonderful, why doesn't it answer my questions?"

4. Our Amazing Listening God 63
   Five minutes a day that will revolutionize your life

5. Signs, Circumstances, and the Will of God 85
   Why putting out the fleece may leave you all wet

6. Who Speaks for God? 101
   Three people you should consult before making any major decision

7. To Thine Own Self Be True 123
   How God uses your desires to communicate His direction

Part Three: Obeying the Master's Voice

8. Marriage, Money, and the Will of God 139
   Five principles for discovering the right mate and the perfect job

9. God's Thundering Silence 157

What to do when the Lord refuses to speak

10. The Shepherd's Safety Net 173

What you can know when you make the wrong *decision*

For Further Reflection: Study Questions on God's Will 187

Appendix: Americans' Views on God's Will:

A National Opinion Study 195

Notes 223

Acknowledgments

You would not be holding this book in your hands if it were not for the valuable contribution of a number of individuals. I am particularly indebted to...

Dan Rich, Steve Cobb, and the gifted team at WaterBrook Press who immediately captured the vision for this project.

Ron Lee, Thomas Womack, and Carol Bartley for your invaluable editorial suggestions.

My friends and agents, Sealy Yates and Pete Richardson, for your continuing encouragement in my writing ministry.

The members of First Baptist Church, Wichita Falls, Texas, for the privilege of serving as your undershepherd.

My family—Amy, Julia, and Dorothy—for your undeserved love and unending support.

Above all, you, the reader, for investing your time and money in this volume. I trust you will not be disappointed as we learn how to experience both the comfort and the confidence of knowing God's will.

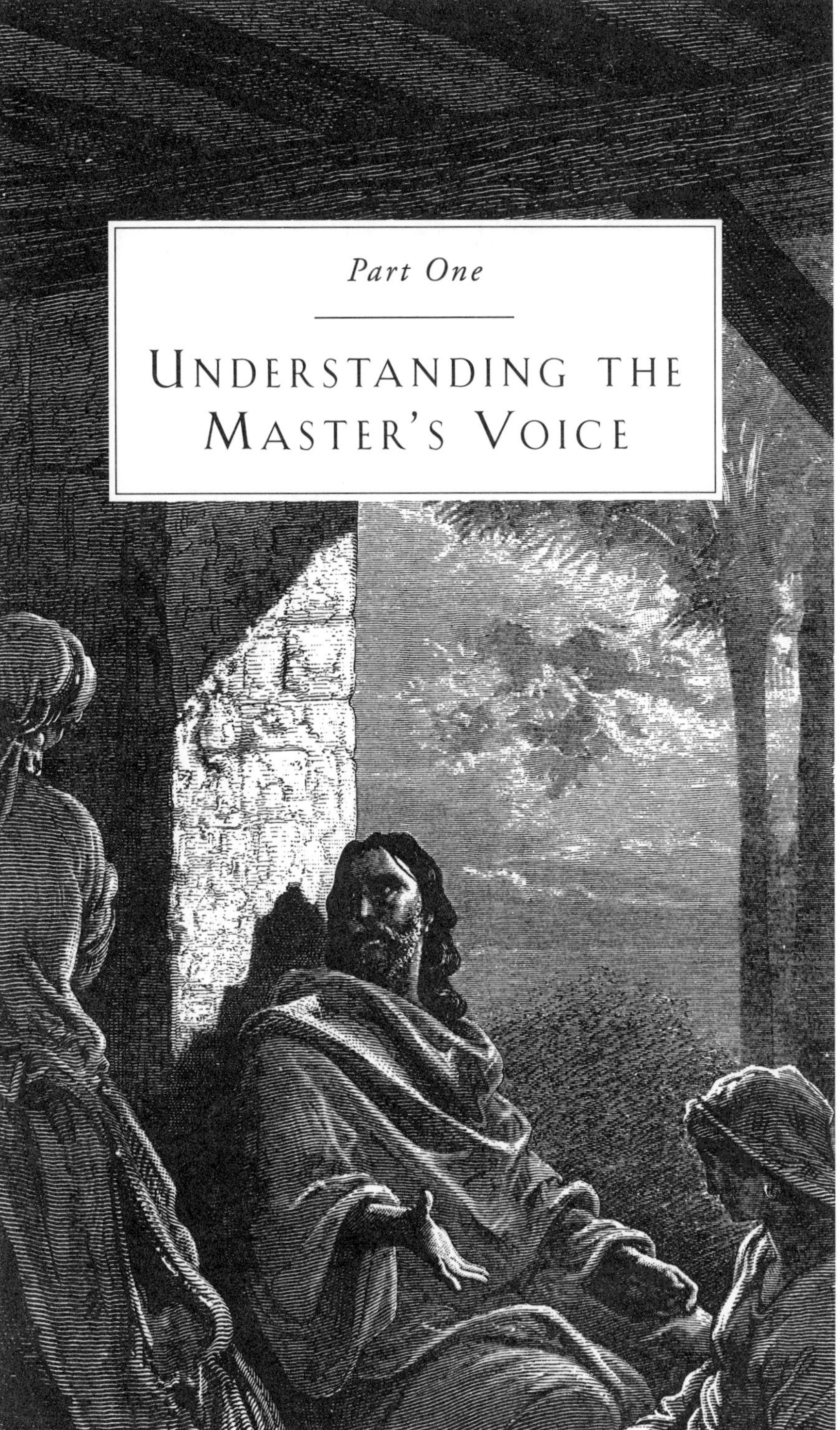

Part One

Understanding the Master's Voice

1

Where There's God's Will, There Must Be a Way

Three common approaches to discovering God's will...
and why they don't work

Bill and Sally Newcomb walked out of their church more confused than they were when they arrived. They were wrestling with a major decision, and what they heard in the sermon that morning did nothing to help clarify their options.

Several weeks earlier Bill had received a phone call from Jerry, a college friend Bill hadn't heard from in years. After spending a few minutes catching up, Jerry got to the real purpose of his call. He'd started an Internet toy business and had heard that Bill was a computer specialist.

"Remember how we used to dream of starting our own business?" Jerry asked. "This is a once-in-a-lifetime opportunity to be your own boss and to get into something on the ground floor that will explode in the next few years."

For the next forty-five minutes Jerry described his vision for the company, occasionally interjecting stories about the gazillion dollars other people had made in similar ventures.

"So, Bill, what do you think?" Jerry asked, hoping to close the sale.

"I'm not sure, Jerry. This is all so sudden. I need to talk things over with Sally and pray about it. How soon do you need an answer?"

"It's important that we move quickly. Our investors are getting nervous, and I need to have my number-two man in place before I can make some other key decisions. Would two weeks be long enough for you to think it over?"

Bill promised to get back to Jerry with his decision. He was stunned—and excited. For the past twenty years he'd been a systems analyst at the same firm. He earned a comfortable salary that enabled Sally to stay home with their youngest child and work as a volunteer in their church's ministry to underprivileged kids. Nevertheless, Bill had been feeling restless about his job. He'd reached the upper tier of middle management and knew that his chances for further promotion were limited.

Beyond that, he and Sally had been discussing the tremendous financial needs that would confront them in a few years: a college education for three children, the possibility of long-term nursing home care for Sally's mother, and their own retirement. The financial pressure of raising three kids hadn't allowed them the luxury of putting away much money for any of these future needs.

The Newcombs discussed the possibility of changing jobs, and they began to wonder if Jerry's out-of-the-blue offer might be God's way of providing for their family's financial needs. They thought it more than coincidental that when they opened their church's weekly newsletter they noticed that their pastor's next sermon topic would be "How God Speaks." They arrived at church the following Sunday anxious for God to direct them in their pressing decision.

Sitting in their usual pew, Bill and Sally held hands and prayed silently for clear direction. As their pastor spoke, they felt that every word was directed at them. Dr. Fletcher said that knowing God's will was not nearly as difficult as some people believed. "God is much more interested in your knowing His will than even you are. And He communicates His will to us in three primary ways." The pastor then elaborated on the three methods God uses to communicate His plan to us: the Bible, circumstances, and our inward desires. He closed his message with a story about New Testament scholar F. B. Meyer.

"Dr. Meyer was on a ship sailing from England to Ireland. In the middle of the night, as the ship entered the harbor, all that could be seen was a confusing array of lights. Dr. Meyer wondered how the captain could ever hope to navigate into the harbor safely with such a confusing jumble of lights. So he asked the captain about it.

"'You see, sir, it's really quite simple. Do you see that big light over to the left? And do you see that other big light to the right of it? And now, do you see that light still farther this way? Well now, keep your eyes on those three lights and see what happens.'

"As Dr. Meyer watched, the big outer light on the left gradually moved in until it coincided with the middle one. Then, as the ship turned, the combined light gradually merged into the third. 'There now,' said the captain. 'All I have to do is to see that those three big lights become one; then I go straight forward.'

"And so it is with God's will," the pastor concluded. "He has given us three lights to guide us: Scripture, circumstances, and desires. And when those three line up as one, we are free to move ahead."

On the way home, Bill and Sally discussed what they had heard. They agreed that God must care about their decision. After all, the ramifications of their moving would affect their children, their friends, their church, and countless other people. They also accepted their pastor's teaching about the "three lights" God uses to reveal His will. The problem was in determining whether those three indicators—Scripture, circumstances, and desires—were now "in line" to signal a job change for Bill.

FLICKERING LIGHTS

With the future welfare of their family hanging in the balance, there was no room for guesswork. So Bill and Sally decided to look at their career opportunity within the "three lights" framework of God's Word, circumstances, and personal desires. But doing so raised a number of questions. For example, the strongest argument in favor of moving was the potential of increased income to finance their family's future needs. They wondered what the Bible says about higher income as a motivating factor in changing jobs. Recently Bill and Sally had been studying 1 Timothy, and Sally recalled some of Paul's words about the need to be content. She read the verses to Bill: "For we have brought nothing into the world, so we cannot take anything out of it either. And if we have food and covering, with these we shall be content. But those who want to get rich fall into temptation and a snare and many foolish and harmful desires which plunge men into ruin and destruction" (1 Timothy 6:7-9).

"On the other hand," Bill said, "remember what the Bible says about the importance of providing for our family's needs: 'But if anyone does not provide for his own, and especially for those of his household, he has denied the faith, and is worse than an unbeliever' (1 Timothy 5:8). Neither one of us is trying to get rich. We just want to take care of our family, and this new job may be a way to do that."

After recalling some other verses dealing with money, they agreed that the Bible's guiding light on this subject was clouded at best, so they moved to the second beacon: circumstances. Jerry's phone call came completely out of the blue. Wasn't that a sign from God? On the other hand, Sally reminded Bill of several other offers he'd received in the past few years. The fact that he and Jerry had been college roommates and consequently had mutual friends who might have tipped Jerry off about Bill's restlessness made the phone call seem less than miraculous. The circumstances could be read in a variety of ways.

What about the third guiding light their pastor mentioned: inner desires? Bill was finding it increasingly difficult to drag himself out of bed every morning to do a job that had lost its challenge. Sally liked the idea of moving to a new city, purchasing and decorating a new home, and establishing new friendships. But were their desires for change really from God or were they symptomatic of the same midlife malaise that already had descended on many of their friends?

The problem with the three-lights approach was that the signals could be interpreted in a number of ways. Sure, the Bible had a lot to say about financial security, but which passages applied to their particular situation? And when it came to circumstances, were they to view every unsolicited job offer as a sign from God? If so, did that mean God wanted them to move every few years? And then there were their internal desires. It's true that the Bible declares: "Delight yourself in the LORD; [a]nd He will give you the desires of your heart" (Psalm 37:4). But the Bible also says, "The heart is more deceitful than all else [a]nd is desperately sick; [w]ho can understand it?" (Jeremiah 17:9).

There had to be a more reliable way to hear God's voice, if only someone would show them how.

FREEDOM TO CHOOSE

Like the Newcombs, Rachel Jenkins desperately wanted to hear God's voice. But she'd been questioning whether there really was any voice to be heard. Not that she doubted the existence of God, just His interest in the most pressing decision she'd ever faced—whether to marry Roger.

Rachel and Roger met five years ago in a college English class. The attraction was mutual but not explosive. Several months passed before they started dating one another exclusively. The more they talked, the more they realized how much they had in common. Both of them came from small towns, both were committed Christians, and both were willing to wait for God's choice of a marriage partner. Rachel was especially determined not to rush into anything, given her parents' strong admonitions over the years.

For as long as Rachel could remember, her parents had told her they were praying for the boy she would someday marry. This made a profound impression on Rachel as she realized that somewhere out there was just one Mr. Right. If she weren't extremely careful she could get stuck with Mr. Wrong. And given the Bible's teaching against divorce, she'd be stuck for a lifetime.

Was Roger the man for whom Rachel's parents had been praying? He seemed to fit the description, but how could she know for sure? Like Bill and Sally Newcomb, Rachel had heard all about the three lights God was said to use in disclosing His will. But when it came to responding to Roger's proposal of marriage, the lights had all gone dim. While the Bible clearly taught that she should marry a Christian, it failed to provide the man's first and last name. There were no unusual circumstances surrounding their meeting that would indicate it was a heavenly appointment. And as for the third guiding light, Rachel was having trouble reading her own deepest desires. She was excited about the possibility of marrying Roger. But were those desires synonymous with God's direction, or were they simply the normal impulses of a twenty-three-year-old single woman? There must be a better way to discern God's will.

Rachel mentioned her dilemma to a friend, who recommended a book on the subject of discovering God's will. The book claimed that God isn't in the divine matchmaker business. Instead, He has a sovereign will that is known only to Him. He also has a moral will that gives us boundaries for our decision making. But God has no individual blueprint for every choice we confront.

As an example, the book asked, "Does God have a will regarding the kind of car we drive? Does He prefer Fords to Pontiacs? Do we need to pray about whether to order a hamburger or a hot dog for lunch? Of course not! God has given His children a great deal of latitude in decision making." Our responsibility, according to the book, is to know the scriptural principles that form a boundary around our decisions and then concentrate on making the wisest decision we can.

Rachel was liberated by this revolutionary concept. No longer did she have to struggle under the weight of finding the one Mr. Right in the entire universe. God had left the choice up to her as long as she stayed within His established boundaries. Roger was a committed Christian, which seemed to be the only biblical principle involved. As far as wise decision making goes, their similar backgrounds and interests seemed to give their potential marriage a better-than-average chance of success. Her parents approved of Roger and promised their blessing on the marriage.

But this newfound freedom in decision making began to haunt Rachel as her wedding day approached. Was it really true that the same God who numbered every hair on her head had no preference regarding her choice of a life partner? What about the scriptural command not to worry about anything but to pray about everything? Doesn't the advice to pray presuppose some kind of answer from God? The teaching that God had no individual will for Rachel's life (or at least one that could be discerned) eventually caused her to feel abandoned, not liberated.

The Wrong Answer

Darla Everett was angry with God, and for good reason. She was convinced that He had lied to her, and she didn't know if she ever could trust Him again. Darla discovered she was pregnant long after she and her husband, Mark, had agreed their childbearing years were over. An eight-year-old girl and two teenage boys provided all the activity their household needed. But they eventually warmed to the idea of having another baby. Darla was in her forties, but she would gladly nurture another child.

Then, during a checkup, her excitement turned to concern. Darla's doctor informed her of the physical risks associated with a pregnancy at her age. Abortion was not an option, she informed the doctor. She and Mark were confident that God would take care of their baby.

But that confidence waned over the course of Darla's pregnancy as she faced a series of complications. Several times the doctor advised the amniocentesis procedure to get a reading on the baby's health, but Darla refused. What value would there be in discovering whether the baby was handicapped since they already had ruled out ending the pregnancy?

Several weeks before her due date, Darla was folding laundry when suddenly she was paralyzed by fear. She was certain that something was desperately wrong with her baby. All she knew to do was to cry out to God. "Lord, you know that I'm at a breaking point. I can't stand not knowing if my baby is all right or not. Please, Lord, give me some assurance that everything is all right." Darla felt a strong impulse to turn to a familiar and well-marked Scripture passage. She read the words aloud as if she were reading them for the first time:

For Thou didst form my inward parts;
Thou didst weave me in my mother's womb.
I will give thanks to Thee, for I am fearfully and wonderfully made;
Wonderful are Thy works,

And my soul knows it very well....
Thine eyes have seen my unformed substance;
And in Thy book they were all written,
The days that were ordained for me,
When as yet there was not one of them. (Psalm 139:13-14,16)

As she closed her Bible, Darla believed she heard God's voice: "Don't worry. I'm in control. Your child is fine." For the next two months, she clung to that assurance. That's why, after her delivery, the doctor's words came as such a devastating shock. "Darla, we're going to do some further testing. But it looks as if your baby has Down syndrome." Darla and Mark were numb. But almost instantaneously, her shock turned to anger. "God, why did You tell me everything was fine and then allow this to happen? How could You do such a thing?"

Several months earlier she had prayed and received an answer. But was it the voice of God that Darla heard that day, or was it simply her own overwhelming desire for a healthy baby? If she was mistaken about that experience, what about the other times she thought she'd heard God speak? Were all those experiences bogus as well?

The challenge of raising a Down syndrome baby was her immediate concern. But eventually Darla knew she'd have to confront the problem of serving a God who at best is difficult to understand and at worst impossible to trust.

A BETTER STRATEGY

With so many conflicting messages telling us how God reveals His will, where can we turn to find a foolproof method? Does God even speak to people today? If so, does He communicate in the same way He did in the Bible? If He wants us to know His will, why is His voice so difficult to discern? What sorts of things does God speak to us about? And how can we distinguish between God's voice and our own strong desires?

If you're a Christian you've probably asked these questions many times. I recently asked my church's media ministry for a list of the most frequently requested sermon tapes. Ranking at the top were messages related to the family, forgiveness, and "how to know God's will for my life." Why is there such interest in this topic? Some cynics might speculate that most people are not so much interested in "God's will" as they are in "my life." People are interested in any help they can get with *my* marriage, *my* job, *my* finances, or *my* goals. In fact, my brother wrote me a four-page letter begging me not to write this book, which he argued was a capitulation to the egocentricity of most Christians. Why feed this obsession with self at the expense of honoring almighty God?

With all due respect to my brother, I can think of three reasons why devoting ourselves to finding God's will isn't an exercise in self-centeredness.

First, when we read the Bible, we see that it's natural for Christians to want to know their Father's will. Consider Jesus' example when He said, "My food is to do the will of Him who sent Me, and to accomplish His work" (John 4:34). Shouldn't every Christian have the same goal as the apostle Paul, who wrote, "Therefore also we have as our ambition, whether at home or absent, to be pleasing to Him" (2 Corinthians 5:9)? It's not egocentric to want to follow God's plan for our lives. Like Jesus and Paul, all true believers have a natural (or more accurately, supernatural) desire to hear God's voice so that we might obey it. And if we are going to please God by obeying His will, we must assume that God has a plan for each of our lives and that we can know what His plan is.

A second reason there is heightened interest in hearing God's voice is the exploding number of options we face for just about every decision we make. I love the story Haddon Robinson tells about the news reporter who was writing an article about the Florida citrus industry. The journalist walked into a plant and saw a man sorting oranges. As the oranges came rolling down the conveyer belt, the worker sorted them according to their size. Large oranges were sent through large holes in the sorting apparatus, small oranges into small holes, and the bruised oranges into a third set of holes.

The reporter watched the man perform this incredibly boring job until he couldn't stand it any longer. Finally he asked the worker, "How can you stand putting these oranges into those holes all day long?"

"You don't know the half of it," the man said. "From the time I come into work until the time I go home, it's decisions, decisions, decisions!"[1]

Unfortunately, few of us lead lives that are that simple. For just about every decision we face, there are seemingly unlimited options. Our parents were spared this endless array of choices. When they called long distance, they used the one long-distance carrier that was available. If our parents flew to another city, one uniform fare governed the price of seats on all the airlines. And before their time, when Henry Ford rolled out the first U.S. automobile, there was one model and one color available. Today, when buying a car or just about any other consumer goods, we can choose from 25 million different brands, models, colors, and accessory combinations.[2]

The same industrial and technological explosion that provides us with so many consumer options also presents us with choices in other areas of life. Unlike any previous generation, we have seemingly unlimited choices for our occupation, where we live, whom we marry, the type of church we'll attend, and what kind of health treatment we'll receive (or choose not to receive). No wonder today's Christians are so hungry for divine assistance in sorting through the myriad of choices.

But there is a third reason that hearing God's voice is particularly important for Christians today. Ironically, we're intent on finding God's will because of the multitude of human voices telling us the "right" way to hear God. Visit a Christian bookstore or surf the Web (more options again) and you'll find a plethora of books promising to show you the best way to find God's will. The problem is not that no one is addressing this vital topic, but that *so many* are addressing it from seemingly contradictory points of view. The result is greater confusion about an already confusing topic.

Sorting Through the Confusion

Bill and Sally Newcomb, whose story opened this chapter, know the difficulty of finding a method that really does clarify God's will. They wanted to follow God's leading in making a decision about a job offer, so they tried their pastor's "formulaic" approach. Just as an airplane pilot goes through a checklist before proceeding down the runway, God is said to have given us a divine checklist that governs our every decision. On that checklist are the three items mentioned by the Newcombs' pastor: Scripture, circumstances, and personal desires. Additional items might include prayer and the counsel of other Christians.

As we will see later, each of these can be tremendously helpful in making the best decision, but there are also major limitations to this method. What happens when one item contradicts all the others on the checklist? Do you assume that "the majority rules" and go through with the decision? Or do you fail to act since the various indicators weren't unanimous?

My father used to work for a commercial airline and had the responsibility of signing the release forms that cleared the aircraft to fly. Rarely did *everything* on an airplane work, but there were certain items that could be inoperative without preventing the plane from flying safely. A burned-out light in the lavatory didn't warrant the same caution as a leaking fuel line. Every item on the checklist was weighted according to its importance.

The problem with the formulaic approach in discovering God's will is that it doesn't provide a method for weighting the importance of various factors. For example, suppose Bill and Sally are considering their friend's job offer. But instead of offering a position in a new e-commerce company, Jerry had offered Bill the chance to become the head drug lord in another city. Such a career change would violate the truth of Scripture even if Bill and Sally could justify it through circumstances (an unsolicited job offer that addressed Bill's restlessness) and their internal desires for a significant life change (a new town, a new house, a new adventure). The Bible always trumps every other factor in our decision making.

But now back to the real world! The Bible does not address whether Bill and Sally should move to another city to work for an e-commerce company. So they must jump ahead to the next few items on the checklist. Yes, circumstances seem to point toward a change. Yes, they have a desire to make more money and move to a new city. But after talking with a friend who went bankrupt in a similar venture, they are beginning to have second thoughts. Isn't the advice of a trusted fellow believer more valid than an inward impression? The Bible says, "[I]n abundance of counselors there is victory" (Proverbs 24:6). On the other hand, think about Abraham. Did it really make sense for him to leave everything that was familiar to him in order to travel to a country he had never seen? No doubt his friends and family members advised him against leaving a stable environment for an uncertain future.

The formulaic approach is helpful only when all the items on the checklist are in agreement or when the Bible speaks directly for or against an anticipated action. But in the real world of career choices, educational options for our children, and deciding where to live or what church to attend, that seldom happens.

Another approach to discerning God's leading is what I call the "experiential" method. Search the Bible, proponents of this method say, and you don't find God's servants consulting a checklist for direction. Instead, God communicated clearly to those who wanted to know His will. God thundered His commands to Moses on Mount Sinai. He unveiled His plan for Israel's future in a vision to Daniel. He revealed His desire for Paul's ministry through the vision of the man from Macedonia. He whispered His assurance to Elijah in the sound of gentle stillness.

God hasn't changed, we are told. He still speaks to us today if only we will listen. But if we're honest, few of us would claim to have literally heard God's voice. One pastor, being questioned about his call to the ministry, was asked, "Did you hear God speak audibly?" "No," my friend said. "It was stronger than that."

Clever reply, but it raises an important question. Apart from a voice shouting from heaven, how am I to distinguish between God's voice and my own desires? Darla, the mother with the Down syndrome baby, learned the hard way that we can easily confuse personal desires with God's voice. And what happens when I hear nothing from God but still must make a decision? We will give particular attention to this question in future chapters.

A third popular approach to finding divine guidance is the "rational" approach that Rachel encountered when debating whether to marry Roger. According to this view, God has no individual blueprint for our lives regarding whom we are to marry, what vocation we are to choose, or what ministries we are best suited for. Instead of trying to discover some specific will of God, we should concentrate on learning how to make wise decisions. Thus, the real question regarding areas the Bible does not specifically address is not "What is God's will?" but rather "What is the wisest decision I can make?" Proponents of this view say that God is most pleased by our wise decisions. This is such a popular, but flawed, view that we will examine it in depth in the next chapter.

The One Clear Choice

It's easy to see why there is such confusion concerning God's will. But above the clamor of these contradictory messages, we still can hear the simple promise of our Shepherd, Jesus Christ: "My sheep hear My voice, and I know them, and they follow Me" (John 10:27). Notice three characteristics of the Master's voice that we find in that simple sentence.

1. God's voice can be heard. Jesus' promise that we can hear His voice presupposes that He is indeed speaking to us. Jesus assures us that He is there, and that He is not silent.

2. God's voice can be discerned. In John 10, Jesus gives both a condition and a promise. The promise is that those who belong to God can be assured of hearing God. But notice the condition: To hear *from* God we must belong *to* God.

3. God's voice gives direction. His voice is not limited to providing us with courage and comfort. Jesus describes the type of voice that provides guidance so that we might follow the Shepherd. This truth is essential as we consider the challenge of finding God's will for our lives.

Jesus' imagery of the shepherd and his sheep is pregnant with significance. Sheep are infamous for their lack of direction and their strong need for leadership. The Palestinian shepherd was known not only for his love for his sheep, but also for his strong leadership over the flock. He was absolutely determined that the sheep in his care would make it safely from one pasture to another, and he would take whatever steps were necessary to ensure their safe arrival. If a sheep wandered from the fold, the shepherd might sling a rock at the sheep, aimed so that it would land directly in front of the animal without hitting it. Startled by the rock, the sheep would return to the security of the fold.[3]

Most of us are familiar with the verse in Isaiah that says "All of us like sheep have gone astray, [e]ach of us has turned to his own way" (53:6).

That verse often is used to describe unbelievers, but it is also an apt description of Christians. Jesus says that even after we become Christians, we still retain our sheeplike qualities. We have a tendency to get distracted, confused, and enticed by other pastures. But fortunately we have a loving Shepherd who is absolutely resolved to see that we follow the path He has chosen for us.

If God is so committed to revealing His plans to us, why is it so difficult to discern exactly what He wants? One obstacle is the confusion that results from contradictory teachings and beliefs on how God shows us His will.

My publisher commissioned a national opinion study to determine what people believe about God's will. In interviews with a representative sampling of adults across the United States, the Barna Research Group found significant differences in the approaches we use. (See the complete research findings in the appendix at the end of this book.) The study found that many Christians use more than one method to discern God's will. And since respondents weren't asked to select only one approach, the following percentages don't add up to one hundred. But the most popular is the "rational" approach, which is backed by 90 percent of born-again Christians. This method is based on the belief that God grants us wide latitude in decision making, assuming that we take into account the constraints of His moral law. Hence, a person makes a decision based on logically evaluating all the available options. This approach, which also is supported by 77 percent of non-Christians, runs counter to the idea that God has *specific* plans for our lives in areas that are not addressed in the Bible.

The second most popular method, supported by 79 percent of born-again Christians, is the "formulaic" method, which requires that the major indicators of God's will (prayer, Bible reading, counsel, circumstances, and personal feelings) all point to the same answer. This approach creates problems when one or more of the indicators contradict the others.

The third most popular approach, adhered to by 61 percent of born-again Christians, is the "experiential" approach, which looks for some type of supernatural sign from God. Indeed, 64 percent of born-again Christians can recall a time when God revealed His will to them on a specific decision through a dream, sign, vision, voice, or other unusual occurrence. The limitation inherent in this method is that it singles out just one of the many ways God reveals His will.

In spite of the disagreement and confusion surrounding the best way to find God's will, we know that people are eager to discover His plan. The study reveals that 68 percent of all adults, including 57 percent of non-Christians and 83 percent of born-again Christians, are facing a decision for which they "would like to get direction from God." Fortunately, God delights in revealing His desires to us. But He doesn't limit Himself to the three most popular methods cited in this study. In the chapters that follow, we'll discover all of the means that God uses to make His perfect plans clear to us. We'll look at the widely recognized indicators as well as a few methods that have been discredited in some Christian circles. Our guide will be the Bible and what it tells us about God's methods of communicating with us.

If you're like the majority of Americans, you are facing decisions right now for which you need and want God's clear direction. You're ready to follow God, but you first need to know in which direction He is leading. I pray that in the pages that follow you'll discover you have a loving heavenly Father who…

is vitally concerned with *every* step you take,
promises to give you the guidance you need,
and can be clearly heard by those who are truly His.

2

Scrutinizing the Inscrutable

What you can *know and what you will* never *know about God's will for your life*

The great nineteenth-century prayer warrior George Mueller was confident that he had found the key to unlocking the will of God. He claimed he could accurately discern God's will whenever he "sincerely and patiently" sought it "by the teaching of the Holy Ghost, through the instrumentality of the Word of God." Sincerity, patience, and reliance on the Holy Spirit and holy Scripture were Mueller's guarantees of hearing God's voice on important matters of personal concern.[1]

When I first read Mueller's words, I came away less than inspired. All I could think was, *That's great for you, George, but that hasn't been my experience. There have been plenty of times when I begged God to show me what to do and He didn't answer. I was left to fend for myself.*

Not long ago I needed to hire a new staff member for our church. The position was of vital importance, and I certainly wanted God's direction in the matter. I interviewed a number of candidates, checked references, and sought the recommendation of respected colleagues. And above all, I prayed for God's guidance. But after going through all that, I never heard

God say yes or no regarding a particular candidate. Why didn't He speak to me about such an important matter?

On the other hand, I can recall two instances in my life when I heard God speak very clearly. But neither time was I even asking Him to speak. He did so without my permission. (Funny how He has a way of doing that!)

My study of God's Word, coupled with my own experience and that of others I have counseled, has led me to three conclusions about hearing the Master's voice. First, we must desire to hear God's voice. Second, we must recognize that God speaks in a variety of ways. And third, we must realize that God reveals only what we need to know. Let's look at each of these truths in more detail.

We Must Desire to Hear God's Voice

As we saw in the last chapter, true followers of God desire to hear His voice in order to obey His will. Jesus said, "For I have come down from heaven, not to do My own will, but the will of Him who sent Me" (John 6:38). Jesus also said the consuming passion of His life was "to do the will of Him who sent Me, and to accomplish His work" (John 4:34). Is that true for you? When you roll out of bed in the morning, is your first thought, "I wonder how God would have me spend my time today?" When you are faced with a difficult dilemma at work, do you automatically consult God for His direction? When you are trying to help your child make a decision regarding his future, do you pray, "Lord, what is *Your* desire for my child's life?"

While few of us are theological atheists, we often live as practical atheists. We formulate our goals, expend our resources, and confront our dilemmas as if there were no God in heaven who might want to have a say in our affairs. But there *is* a God who delights in our desire to hear His voice. We see that truth illustrated in the life of Solomon at the beginning of his reign as king over Israel.

> In Gibeon the LORD appeared to Solomon in a dream at night; and God said, "Ask what you wish me to give you."
>
> Then Solomon said, "Thou hast shown great lovingkindness to Thy servant David my father, according as he walked before Thee in truth and righteousness and uprightness of heart toward Thee.... And now, O LORD my God, Thou hast made Thy servant king in place of my father David, yet I am but a little child; I do not know how to go out or come in.... So give Thy servant an understanding heart to judge Thy people to discern between good and evil. For who is able to judge this great people of Thine?"
>
> And it was pleasing in the sight of the Lord that Solomon had asked this thing. (1 Kings 3:5-7,9-10)

Solomon was attempting to fill some pretty big shoes left by his father, David. In spite of the palace scandal that had corrupted David's rule in the latter years of his reign, David still left his son with a kingdom that was both prosperous and powerful. Realizing the daunting task that confronted him, Solomon knew he needed to spend some time with God. So in the beginning days of his administration, he took time off from the frantic schedule of kingdom life and traveled to the village of Gibeon to be alone with God. While there, God appeared to Solomon and told him that he could request anything he wanted.

Now think about this for a moment. If you were nineteen or twenty years old, like Solomon, what would *you* ask for? Instead of requesting the latest model chariot, a closet full of designer tunics, or a harem full of beautiful women (that would come later), Solomon asked the Lord to give him "an understanding heart." The word *understanding* in Hebrew means "hearing."

Solomon, above all else, wanted to be able to hear the Master's voice. Why? He tells us in verse 9: "For who is able to judge this great people of Thine?"

Every day the new king would be confronted with numerous dilemmas, each one with multiple options. And it would be up to Solomon to make the right decision. The young man understood that his lack of experience rendered him incapable of making wise decisions by himself. So he asked—he pleaded—with God for the ability to know His will in every situation.

What was God's response? First, let's notice what God *did not* say: "Solomon, why do you think I'd be interested in the day-to-day details of your job? I have bigger concerns to deal with." Nor did He say, "Solomon, I've already given you a mind and My Word. Your responsibility is to make wise decisions." Neither did He respond, "Solomon, since I don't have an individual will for those who will be coming to you for counsel, don't bother asking Me for guidance about the trivial details of life."

No, the Bible records that "it was pleasing in the sight of the Lord that Solomon had asked this thing" (1 Kings 3:10). In fact, it was so pleasing that God not only granted Solomon's request for a hearing heart, but He threw in the new chariot, the clothes, and everything else anyone could possibly desire!

Frankly, I'm getting a little tired of the superpious folks who discourage us from asking for God to speak to us about the decisions we face. They would lead us to believe that any request for direction is an affront to God and an affirmation of a self-centered life. "If you were really in tune with the heart of God," they tell us, "you'd know that He is much more interested in His glory than the mundane affairs of your everyday life."

Yet God's Word draws no such dichotomy between our lives and God's glory. It is in the choices we make every day that God's name is either exalted or debased. And that is why the Bible continually encourages us to seek God's guidance for our life. Consider these commands and promises:

> Trust in the LORD with all your heart, [a]nd do not lean on your own understanding. In all your ways acknowledge Him, [a]nd He will make your paths straight. (Proverbs 3:5-6)
>
> But if any of you lacks wisdom, let him ask of God, who gives to all men generously and without reproach, and it will be given to him. (James 1:5)
>
> I urge you therefore, brethren, by the mercies of God, to present your bodies a living and holy sacrifice, acceptable to God, which is your spiritual service of worship. And do not be conformed to this world, but be transformed by the renewing of your mind, that you may prove what the will of God is, that which is good and acceptable and perfect. (Romans 12:1-2)

Notice the high value that God places on seeking His guidance. He is pleased when we desire to know His will. When we sincerely ask for His wisdom, God promises to honor our request for direction.

But exactly how does God speak to us regarding the matters that concern us most? Before we answer that question, it's important to distinguish between the various meanings of the "will of God."

Three Dimensions of God's Will

Years ago when I served as a youth minister, I regularly asked our youth group to identify the topics they were most interested in hearing about.

The hands-down winner was always "sex and dating" or "dating and sex" or some variation thereof. The youth minister at our church tells me that still holds true.

The second most popular topic was always "how to know God's will for my life." These adolescents were being bombarded with big decisions for which they sincerely sought divine direction: Whom should I date? What college should I attend? What major should I choose? Those are crucial questions for young people. But before I addressed God's method for communicating direction about those legitimate questions, I always differentiated between the three possible meanings of the phrase "the will of God."

God's Providential Will

God has a hidden plan that controls everything that happens in this universe. For the most part, this plan is incomprehensible to our finite minds. Occasionally, though, God may choose to reveal this hidden plan to us. For example, in Ephesians 1:9 Paul writes: "He made known to us the mystery of His will, according to His kind intention which He purposed in Him."

God had decided before the creation of the world that He would one day send His Son to die for the yet uncreated human race. But that sovereign purpose of God was revealed to us according to God's timetable, not ours.

There are other parts of God's providential will that are completely hidden from us. This would include such mysteries as predestination, the origin of evil, and the reasons for suffering. The Bible says about such matters that "[t]he secret things belong to the LORD" (Deuteronomy 29:29).

Not only is God's providential will mostly hidden from us, but it is also unchangeable (the theological term is *immutable*). That is, God's providential will is going to be accomplished with or without our cooperation.

When Peter preached his sermon at Pentecost in Jerusalem he was addressing the very people who, a few weeks earlier, had crucified Jesus Christ. Nevertheless, Peter said that Christ's death was not a tragedy that caught God by surprise: "[T]his Man, delivered up by the predetermined plan and foreknowledge of God, you nailed to a cross by the hands of godless men and put Him to death" (Acts 2:23).

Yes, these Jews and Romans who drove the nails through Christ's flesh would one day answer to God for what they had done. However, their actions were a part of God's providential will, His predetermined plan that would not and could not be thwarted.

While it might be interesting to understand the imponderables of God's providential plan, the Bible never encourages us to do so. In fact, as Job found out, God discourages us from trying to "unscrew the inscrutable." Understandably perplexed over the tremendous loss he had experienced, Job questioned God about the whys of suffering. In response, God basically said, "Job, in a thousand lifetimes you could never understand what I am up to. Trust Me, I know what I'm doing."

Eventually Job came to the same conclusion about God's providential will: "I know that you can do anything, and no one can stop you. You ask, 'Who is this that questions my wisdom with such ignorance?' It is I. And I was talking about things I did not understand, things far too wonderful for me" (Job 42:2-3, NLT).

God's Preceptive Will

On the other end of the spectrum, there is an aspect of God's will that is completely comprehensible to all of us: God's preceptive will. I am referring to God's desire for our lives that is set forth in the Bible. Sometimes these precepts, or commands, are general principles that give us specific direction. For example, Paul wrote, "For this is the will of God, your sanctification; that is, that you abstain from sexual immorality; that each of you know how to possess his own vessel in sanctification and honor" (1 Thessalonians 4:3-4).

In the "sex and dating" discussions with teenagers, one of the frequently asked questions was "How far can we go without sinning?" While the Bible doesn't give a detailed answer to that question, there is a general principle that should govern our behavior: We are to abstain from any immoral behavior.

Here's another example. Last week a church member called me and said, "I'm wondering whether it's the right time to share the gospel with a friend in my aerobics class. She seems open, but I don't want to take advantage of our friendship and ruin any further chances I might have to witness to her." The woman who called was not afraid of sharing the gospel, but she simply had a question about timing. I pointed her to some closing verses in 2 Peter 3:

> The Lord is not slow about His promise, as some count slowness, but is patient toward you, not wishing for any to perish but for all to come to repentance. But the day of the Lord will come like a thief, in which the heavens will pass away with a roar...and the earth and its works will be burned up. (vv. 9-10)

It is God's clear desire that everyone should be saved, Peter wrote. Therefore, I took this general principle and encouraged my parishioner to share the gospel with her friend since there is no guarantee of tomorrow.

Sometimes God's preceptive will is very specific. For example, the businessman who wonders whether he should cosign a bank loan for a friend doesn't need to pray and fast in order to sense God's leading. God already has spoken about the matter, saying, "A man lacking in sense pledges, [a]nd becomes surety in the presence of his neighbor" (Proverbs 17:18).

Similarly, the single adult who wonders whether she should marry that successful, moral man who, unfortunately, is not yet a Christian ("but is really close to making a decision") need not wonder what God's will might be. He has already told us: "Do not be bound together with unbelievers; for what partnership have righteousness and lawlessness, or what fellowship has light with darkness?" (2 Corinthians 6:14). In many instances, the answers to our dilemmas can be found in the general or specific precepts given in God's Word. It is presumptuous to believe that God is going to give us new revelation (or worse, *different* revelation) about a question He has already addressed.

God's Personal Will

We most commonly use the term *God's will* to refer to God's individual plan for our own lives. We want to know His mind in the matters of selecting a mate, a career, a geographical location, and many more major life concerns. But does God actually have such a specific plan for our lives? And if so, can we know exactly what that plan is?

A number of years ago Garry Friesen wrote a helpful but controversial book called *Decision Making and the Will of God.* According to Friesen, God has a sovereign will that we can see clearly only after the fact. God also has a moral will that is revealed in Scripture. But Friesen insists that God has no individual will for our lives that governs our everyday decisions. Instead, he proposes, God wants us to learn to make wise decisions according to the general principles outlined in Scripture. If we believe that God does have a blueprint for every aspect of our lives, Friesen argues, why don't we seek God's guidance for what we have for breakfast as well as the identity of our future mate?

Since I differ with Friesen on that last point, I'll offer two lines of defense for the concept of an individual will of God for each of us.

The logical argument. It simply doesn't make sense that God has no particular design for the details of our lives. Consider the precision with which He designed our universe. The earth is tilted on a twenty-three-degree axis. If you believe God doesn't care about such details, consider what would happen if the angle were twenty-seven degrees. Part of the earth would burn up and the rest would be frozen solid.

Here's another example. The atmosphere is composed of 21 percent oxygen. Is God interested in such trivia? What if the percentage were to climb to, say, 50 percent? At that level, the first time someone lit a match the whole atmosphere would go up in flames!

Now let's get a little more personal. Is it logical to assume that God had no preference in the matter of whom your father married? Before you answer too quickly, read the psalm that Darla Everett stumbled upon when she was seeking to hear God's voice about the health of her unborn child:

> For Thou didst form my inward parts;
> Thou didst weave me in my mother's womb.
> I will give thanks to Thee, for I am fearfully and wonderfully made;
> Wonderful are Thy works,
> And my soul knows it very well....
> Thine eyes have seen my unformed substance;
> And in Thy book they were all written,
> The days that were ordained for me,
> When as yet there was not one of them. (Psalm 139:13-14,16)

The Hebrew word translated *weave* in verse 13 refers to the interweaving of a large vine. The psalmist is saying that while we were in our mother's womb, God wove together all of our physical, emotional, and spiritual attributes into one complex creation. Nothing was left to chance. Everything was by divine design.

I am no geneticist, but I know just enough to draw this simple conclusion. If God has a predetermined design for every aspect of your body—green eyes, brown hair, birthmark on the right cheek, crooked index finger—then He has a definite idea of who your father should marry. There is only one man and one woman who could join together to produce a child with your unique DNA code.

Not only that, but the psalmist also declares that every detail of your life *after* birth was written in God's book before you even drew your first breath. Is it logical to assume that when God sat down to plan the course of your life, He simply shrugged His shoulders and wrote "whatever" in the blanks labeled "Names of Parents" and "Identity of Future Mate"?

The biblical argument. Since logic can't always be trusted to understand spiritual truth, we should see if the Bible says anything about God's personal will for our lives. Admittedly, some of the passages that use the phrase *God's will* deal with His providential or preceptive will. But other times, this phrase is a definite reference to a unique plan God has for each individual life.

Several years ago I took a group to Israel to retrace the steps of Jesus. We visited the supposed site of the Nativity, sailed the Sea of Galilee, gazed at Golgotha, and sang in front of the empty tomb. But one of the most moving experiences was kneeling in the Garden of Gethsemane—the very place where our eternal destiny was decided.

Make no mistake about it. Jesus did not want to experience the physical and spiritual trauma of crucifixion. The decision to go to Calvary and endure God's wrath on our behalf didn't come easily. Luke tells us that Jesus was in great agony over this decision, to the point that His pores emitted what appeared to be drops of blood.

> "Father, if Thou art willing, remove this cup from Me; yet not My will, but Thine be done."... And being in agony He was praying very

> fervently; and His sweat became like drops of blood, falling down upon the ground. (Luke 22:42,44)

Jesus had a personal preference about going to the cross: He didn't want to go (v. 42). But He realized that God also had a will in the matter. The will to which Jesus ultimately acquiesced was not some general preceptive will that applied to every believer. No, Jesus was obedient to a different category of God's will—the Father's personal blueprint for Christ's life, which included Calvary.

"Well," some would say, "it may be true that God had a personal blueprint for Jesus' life, but after all, He was the Son of God. Is there any other evidence that God has a specific will for my life?" Yes, in fact there is.

Consider Paul's experience with the church at Rome. The apostle had desired for years to visit these Christians but had been providentially hindered from doing so. Nevertheless, he continued to pray that "by the will of God I may succeed in coming to you" (Romans 1:10). Did God have any preference whether Paul went to Rome, or did He simply leave that decision to the apostle, hoping he would make a wise decision? Paul declares that the only way he would ever get to Rome was if such a trip were included in God's personal blueprint for his life. (Interestingly, God did allow Paul eventually to go to Rome—not as a preacher but as a prisoner.)

This same apostle also taught that God has an individual will for each of our lives—a will that we should seek to discover so that we might obey it:

> Therefore be careful how you walk, not as unwise men, but as wise, making the most of your time, because the days are evil. So then do not be foolish, but understand what the will of the Lord is. (Ephesians 5:15-17)

Realizing how limited our time on this planet is, Paul says that we should use our time wisely. And one way we can do that is by understanding God's will for our life.

What does Paul mean by "the will of the Lord"? Obviously he is not referring to God's providential plan, since we cannot possibly understand it. Nor is he referring exclusively to God's preceptive or moral will since there is no logical connection between time management and morality. Does saying no to adultery help you manage your time more efficiently?

Clearly Paul is encouraging us to understand God's personal will so that we can order our lives accordingly. As the prophet Jonah discovered, resisting God's personal plan for our lives can result in wasted days and waterlogged feet.

God Speaks in a Variety of Ways

I doubt that you have trouble believing that God has an individual plan for your life. Instinctively you know that the same God who has numbered the hairs on your head probably has some thoughts about where you should live, whom you should marry, and what job should consume the majority of your waking hours.

The real question is not "Does God have a plan for my life?" but "How can I know God's plan for my life?" The latter is the focus of the remainder of this book.

To understand how God speaks today it might be helpful to review how God has communicated to His people in the past. If God is the same yesterday, today, and forever, is it illogical to assume that He might employ the same communication methods that have served Him so well in the past? Let's consider some of the ways God spoke to His people in the past.

The Written Word

It is extremely significant that when God called Moses to the top of Mount Sinai to receive a message for the people of Israel, God did not communicate His message through a vision that Moses would in turn relate to the people. Instead, He wrote down His will for the people. God said to Moses:

> "Come up to Me on the mountain and remain there, and I will give you the stone tablets with the law and the commandment which I have written for their instruction."…
>
> And when He had finished speaking with him upon Mount Sinai, He gave Moses the two tablets of the testimony, tablets of stone, written by the finger of God. (Exodus 24:12; 31:18)

Chuck Swindoll explains the significance of this incident this way: The first thing God gave to this man who met with Him was His truth in written form. He took the time to inscribe it in stone. He broke off a chunk of Sinai granite, honed it down so Moses could handle it, and chiseled His revelation into it with His own finger.[2]

Don't ever fall into the trap of thinking that God's written Word is somehow a secondary means for discovering His will. The Bible is God's preferred method of communication. But it's not His *only* method.

Prayer

James promises that any time we lack wisdom we can request it from God, knowing that He will give it to us generously (1:5). When the eleven apostles met together to select the replacement for Judas, they nominated two possible successors with equally impressive qualifications. They firmly believed that God had one perfect choice to fill the position, so they prayed:

> Thou, Lord, who knowest the hearts of all men, show which one of these two Thou hast chosen to occupy this ministry and apostleship from which Judas turned aside to go to his own place. (Acts 1:24-25)

Obviously, when the apostles finished their prayer they still had to make a decision (and how they made that decision will be explored in a later chapter), but don't miss the point. These eleven men who had studied Jesus' every move for three years knew from their observation of His life that God communicates His will to us through prayer.

Special Revelation

The Bible contains many examples of God directly and supernaturally communicating His message through dreams, visions, an audible voice, or a direct revelation of Himself. Consider Paul's experience on the road to Damascus. Paul, formerly called Saul, was an unbeliever intent on traveling to the Syrian capital to exterminate the church of God. But God had a different plan for Saul:

> And it came about that as he journeyed, he was approaching Damascus, and suddenly a light from heaven flashed around him; and he fell to the ground, and heard a voice saying to him, "Saul, Saul, why are you persecuting Me?" (Acts 9:3-4)

Christ not only revealed His identity to Paul that day, but He also communicated His plan for the remainder of Paul's life:

> But arise, and stand on your feet; for this purpose I have appeared to you, to appoint you a minister and a witness not only to the things which you have seen, but also to the things in which I will appear to you; delivering you from the Jewish people and from the Gentiles, to whom I am sending you, to open their eyes so that they may turn from darkness to light and from the dominion of Satan to God. (Acts 26:16-18)

While there certainly are dangers related to relying on special revelation to determine God's will, it is foolish to assume that God is no longer capable or willing to communicate in this way.

Wise Counsel

As I write these words, our church is in the process of installing an image magnification system (big screen televisions) to enhance our worship services. What kind of projectors should we purchase? What kind of computer do we need to control those projectors? Where should we place the screens? Does God care about any of this? I have to believe He does, since this system will assist our people in worshiping Him. But how can we know God's will about these issues?

Obviously, the Bible gives no direct answer to these questions. We certainly are praying for guidance. But unless He appears in a vision by next Wednesday at noon, we'll have to make a decision. Fortunately, God has given us another way for discerning His direction: wise counselors (Proverbs 15:22). Instead of trying to muddle through the decisions ourselves, why not hire a consultant who specializes in big screens for churches or call some other congregations who have been through this and seek their advice? In chapter 6 we will examine in detail how God uses the advice of others to communicate His direction to us.

Circumstances

Sometimes God speaks His will through circumstances, often in the form of open or closed doors. Admittedly, circumstances aren't always definitive. Nevertheless, we shouldn't totally discount their importance. Paul apparently interpreted certain circumstances as indicating God's will. (See the earlier discussion of his attempts to visit Rome.) In Acts 20 we find that Paul was about to travel to Syria when he learned that the Jews were plotting against his life.

> [A]nd when a plot was formed against him by the Jews as he was about to set sail for Syria, he determined to return through Macedonia. (v. 3)

Paul interpreted negative circumstances as positive direction from God.

Desires

Many people are surprised to learn that God often speaks to us through our own desires. Yet Philippians 2:13 assures us that it is "God who is at work within you, giving you the will and the power to achieve his purpose" (Phillips). Your dream of owning your own business, your preference for tall rather than short men, your desire to preach God's Word, or your fear of speaking to large groups—all may be ways God is using to guide you. Obviously, not all of our desires can be attributed to the Almighty. Nevertheless, the Shakespearean admonition to "know thyself" is relevant to hearing the Master's voice.

Perhaps the biggest error many Christians make in hearing God's voice is assuming that He only communicates through one of these methods. The truth is that God speaks to us in a variety of ways. As C. S. Lewis wrote, "I don't doubt that the Holy Spirit guides your decisions from within when you make them with the intention of pleasing God. The error would be to think that He speaks only within, whereas in reality he speaks also through Scripture, the Church, Christian friends, books, etc."[3]

Which leads to a final thought...

God Reveals Only What We Need to Know

Our church once hired a business consultant who met with our staff for several days. He told us that the most important word for any executive was the word *next.* A successful executive doesn't have the answer to every question or the plans for every situation, but he always knows what to do next. The same is true for every believer. God rarely allows us to see every step we need to take for the remainder of our lives, but He will always reveal the next step we need to take.

Sometimes I have wondered why God doesn't just go ahead and reveal His entire plan for our lives in one fell swoop. Perhaps He knows that such a revelation would paralyze us with fear. Looking back on my life, I'm not sure I would have wanted advance knowledge of every disappointment (or for that matter, surprise) I have experienced. As Jesus said, "Each day has enough trouble of its own" (Matthew 6:34).

Or possibly God knows that a complete knowledge of His plan would lessen our dependence on Him. When I'm driving in a thick fog that allows me to see only a few feet in front of the car, I travel much slower than I do when driving on a bright, cloudless day. Our heavenly Father desires that we slow down and derive our direction from Him.

While God never reveals everything we want to know about our future, He promises to communicate the *next* thing we need to know. The psalmist said, "Thy word is a lamp to my feet, [a]nd a light to my path" (Psalm 119:105). Maybe you have walked in the woods on a moonless night with only the aid of a lantern or flashlight. Those instruments do not have enough power to illuminate your path for the next several miles. Instead, they provide just enough light to help you take the next step.

So it is with the voice of God. If you are depending on this book to answer every question you have about your future, then you might as well return this book and invest your money in a pair of dice or some high-quality tea leaves. However, if you desperately desire to know what step God wants you to take next, I believe the following pages will be extremely helpful.

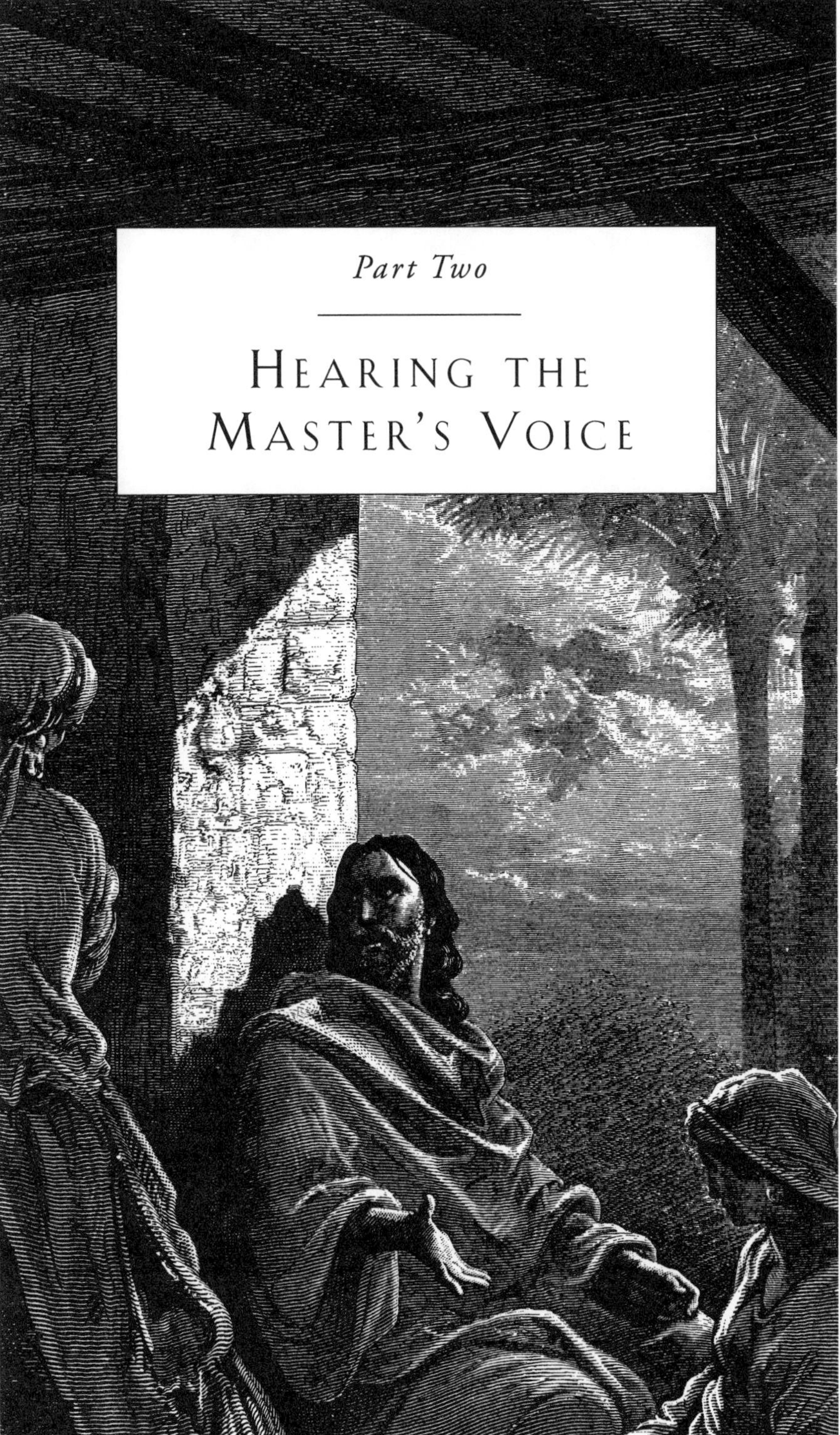

Part Two

HEARING THE MASTER'S VOICE

3

The Bible Tells Me So?

"If the Bible is so wonderful, why doesn't it answer my questions?"

This week marks the anniversary of a milestone in my life. It wasn't the birth of a child or the start of a new job, but a tragedy.

Fourteen years ago, on a Monday evening in Breckenridge, Texas, I was preparing to deliver a sermon at a church conference. As I awaited my turn in the pulpit, I felt a tap on my shoulder. An usher said there was an urgent phone call for me in the church office. I assumed that someone in my congregation had died and that my secretary needed to let me know, though I couldn't understand why she would interrupt me just as I was preparing to preach.

As I made my way to the office, the usher told me the call was from my brother-in-law. My pace picked up considerably as I realized the emergency was not pastoral, but personal. My mother was having exploratory surgery in a Dallas hospital, and the rest of the family was there. I had spoken with her on the phone a few days earlier, and she insisted that I keep my preaching engagement instead of coming to the hospital.

"Robert, it's bad," my brother-in-law said. "There's a malignancy on Judy's liver. The doctor says she has no more than six months to live. Everyone is devastated. You'd better come."

In spite of an overwhelming desire to race out of the church and head for Dallas, I returned to the sanctuary and preached my message, though I have no idea what I said. As soon as the benediction began, my wife and I exited quickly and began the three-hour drive to my parents' home in Dallas.

As tears cascaded down my face, I asked the Lord the same question we all have asked in similar situations: "Why?" Why would God take away a fifty-six-year-old mother and grandmother who was so needed by her family? Why would God allow cancer to silence the strong witness of this Christian schoolteacher who had touched the lives of thousands of children? Why had the doctors missed all the earlier symptoms of colon cancer? A dozen other questions flooded my mind as I raced through the back roads of West Texas.

And then God answered my questions. There was no sudden illumination of the night sky, but there was a voice. I'm not talking about an impression, but an audible voice. It came from my car radio. A well-known Bible teacher was reading from Romans 11:

> Oh, the depth of the riches both of the wisdom and knowledge of God! How unsearchable are His judgments and unfathomable His ways! For who has known the mind of the Lord, or who became His counselor? Or who has first given to Him that it might be paid back to Him again? For from Him and through Him and to Him are all things. To Him be the glory forever. Amen. (vv. 33-36)

As I listened, it was as if God Himself were sitting beside me in the car saying, "I know you don't understand what is happening, but trust Me. I'm in control. I know what I'm doing." On that crisp fall night so many years ago, I heard the Master's voice emanating from the most logical but often overlooked source: the Bible.

How God Reveals Himself

I love the story about the atheist who went mountain climbing. He was making great progress until his feet slipped and he started sliding down a steep slope toward his death. On the way down he grabbed hold of a fragile tree branch. Realizing that the branch wouldn't hold him forever, the atheist looked up and shouted in desperation, "Is there anyone up there who can help me?" "Yes," a voice thundered from heaven. "But you must let go of the tree branch before I can help." After a long pause, the atheist looked up again and called out, "Is there anyone *else* up there who can help me?"

Many of us are searching for a word from God concerning a myriad of subjects, forgetting (or overlooking) the fact that God already has communicated His thoughts to us in the Bible. Dr. Bruce Waltke is correct when he writes:

> Some Christians want to hear the voice of God speaking to them, and I'm telling you that He is already there and He has spoken. King Solomon, the wisest man apart from Jesus who ever walked this earth, encourages us to study God's wisdom in Proverbs: "Bind them upon your heart forever; fasten them around your neck. When you walk, they will guide you; when you sleep, they will watch over you; when you awake, they will speak to you" (Proverbs 6:21-22, NIV). God will talk to you through Scriptures you have memorized.[1]

If God has already spoken, then why do so many Christians look up into heaven and say, "But don't You have anything *else* to say?" Many believers fail to appreciate the uniqueness of the Bible. Specifically, they fail to understand three essential truths about the Scriptures: (1) The Bible is God's perfect revelation; (2) the Bible is God's complete revelation; and (3) the Bible is God's living revelation. When we gain a proper understanding of these truths, we put ourselves in a much better place to hear the Master's voice.

The Bible Is God's Perfect Revelation

When I was a sophomore in high school, I felt God's call to the ministry. A few years later I enrolled in a Christian college, where I started leading Bible studies, working at an inner-city mission, and engaging in an intensive Scripture memory program. Then a religion professor almost persuaded me that there were too many errors in the Bible to believe that it was God's perfect revelation. "This book is simply a collection of man's thoughts about God through the ages," this educator told me. "In the Old Testament you find man's lowest idea of God, but in the New Testament you find man's highest idea of God."

After a steady diet of that kind of teaching I began to wonder why I should give my life to proclaiming a book that couldn't be trusted. I quit reading the Bible, lost interest in my evangelism and mission projects, and seriously considered giving up the ministry (and my faith). Fortunately, God led me to a seminary whose gifted professors reinstilled in me a confidence in the integrity of the Bible.

How can we know the Bible can be trusted as God's perfect revelation to us? First, consider what the Bible claims about itself: "All Scripture is inspired by God and profitable for teaching, for reproof, for correction, for training in righteousness" (2 Timothy 3:16). The word translated "inspired" is the Greek word *theospnuestos* or literally, "God-breathed." All the words of the Bible, Paul claims, came directly from the mouth of God. And as one sage observes, "God doesn't have bad breath!"

Also consider Peter's claim about the divine origin of the Bible: "[F]or no prophecy was ever made by an act of human will, but men moved by the Holy Spirit spoke from God" (2 Peter 1:21). When Paul wrote his epistles, he didn't just awaken in his jail cell and decide, *It's really boring around here. I think I'll write some Scripture to help pass the time.* Likewise, the first five books of the Old Testament were not simply the result of Moses' desire to leave his descendants a detailed "family history." No, Peter says, God is the author of the Bible. Over a period of fifteen hundred years, God carefully guided the work of more than forty writers from various backgrounds (from royalty to fishermen) on three continents to communicate His message, without error, to us.

You may be thinking, *Well, of course, the Bible claims to be God's perfect revelation. You can read glowing endorsements on the back cover of* any *book. So how do I know the Bible's claims about itself can be trusted?* While the scope of this book does not allow a detailed answer to that question, consider just a few of the historical validations of the reliability of the Bible:

> For years critics insisted that the story of Abram's rescue of Lot in Genesis 14 was not historically accurate. They said (1) that the names of the kings listed were fictitious, since they were not independently confirmed in secular histories; (2) that the idea that the king of Babylon was serving the king of Elam was historically impossible; and (3) that the story that a band of Abram's followers could have defeated the united armies of four powerful kings was absurd.
>
> But archaeology has debunked these critics. The names of some of the kings have now been identified. And there is evidence that the king of Babylon did serve the king of Elam at this time. What is more, a monument depicting a warlike expedition of the character described here was discovered, confirming that one tribe pursued another to subdue a rebellion. Abram would have been able to capture Lot and plunder some of the enemy's spoils before a larger army could recoup.

> For decades it was said that the Old Testament writers invented the Hittite tribe, since their existence could not be independently confirmed. However, in 1911-12 Professor Hugo Winkcler of Berlin discovered some ten thousand clay tablets at Bogarzkoy, the site of the Hittite capital. The existence of the Hittite empire is now extensively proven and documented.
>
> The existence of Solomon's reign and his thousands of horses was at one time questioned. But in Megiddo, which was one of five chariot cities, excavations have revealed the ruins of thousands of stalls for his horses and chariots (cf. 1 Kings 10:26-29). Archaeology has also confirmed the disputed reign of Quirinius as governor of Syria at the time of Christ's birth, the existence of the pool of Bethesda (John 5:2), the government service of Pilate, and an altar to "an unknown god" mentioned in Acts 17:23.[2]

There are hundreds of other examples, but I think you get the idea. There is indisputable internal *and* external evidence supporting the Bible's claim that it is God's perfect revelation.

The Bible Is God's Complete Revelation

Even if you accept that the Bible is God's Word, you might question whether it is *all* of God's Word. "What is to keep God from giving me the same kind of special revelation that He gave to Moses, Paul, Peter, and the rest of the biblical authors?" you might ask.

The brief answer is that God can do anything He desires as long as it doesn't contradict His character. If He wanted to, He could awaken you tomorrow morning with His booming voice and say, "I have a brand-new revelation that I want to communicate to My people, and I have chosen to reveal it to *you.* So get out a pen and some paper." The question is not

"*Can* God give additional revelation?" but "*Is* He giving additional revelation today?"

The Scriptures strongly suggest that the Bible is God's final and complete revelation about Himself. For example, Jude wrote to his audience, "Beloved, while I was making every effort to write you about our common salvation, I felt the necessity to write to you appealing that you contend earnestly for the faith which was *once for all* delivered to the saints" (Jude 3).

In that simple verse Jude has said a mouthful. First, there is a body of revealed truth or doctrine called "the faith." Second, this body of truth has already been delivered (the verb translated "delivered" is in a tense that suggests there is no further evidence of continuation). Finally, this truth has been delivered "once for all." That is, there is no additional revealed truth to come.

The writer of Hebrews also asserted that God has voluntarily gotten out of the revelation business. Consider the opening words of Hebrews: "God, after He spoke long ago to the fathers in the prophets in many portions and in many ways, in these last days has spoken to us in His Son, whom He appointed heir of all things, through whom also He made the world" (1:1-2).

Prior to the coming of Jesus Christ, God spoke through a variety of methods ("in many ways"): dreams, visions, an audible voice, and handwriting on the wall, to name a few. Furthermore, He communicated in bits and pieces to the prophets ("in many portions"). No single prophet saw the entire picture. But the writer of Hebrews said that Jesus Christ represents God's complete and final revelation of Himself. Everything you need to know about God you can discover by looking at and listening to His Son: "And He is the radiance of His glory and the exact representation of His nature" (Hebrews 1:3).

There is a difference between God's earlier communication through the Old Testament prophets and His ultimate communication through

Christ. A story from a church I pastored may help illustrate the difference. Members of the congregation occasionally would raise questions about church policy. Invariably a parishioner would say, "We set a policy about that years ago, but I can't remember what it was." Or worse, several people would "remember" the church's policy. Unfortunately, they would have contradictory recollections. Our secretaries would spend hours searching through the minutes of business meetings trying to uncover the church's decision about the issue in question.

I finally got tired of the endless confusion and suggested that we put together an operating handbook. We could incorporate any past policies we wanted to retain, discard the ones that were outdated, and formulate new policies for areas not previously addressed. The church thought it was a great idea, and we developed such a guide. From that point on, anyone who wanted to know the church's policy on a specific issue could find it in the operating guide. The manual was the depository of all the church policies.

Likewise, Jesus Christ is the depository of all the truth about God. You need not look anywhere else to discover what God is like and what He desires from you. And where is there a record of the life and teaching of Jesus Christ? In the Bible. Outside of the Bible, we would know little about Christ and His message (although there are convincing historical references to His life, death, and resurrection). The Bible is the final depository of God's *former* revelation about Himself in the Old Testament and His *final* revelation about Himself in Christ.

The Bible Is God's Living Revelation

Perhaps this is the single characteristic of the Bible that most people miss. You may believe that the *Encyclopedia Britannica* contains accurate information. You may also agree that just about everything you need to know is found within those many volumes. Yet how motivated are you to sit down after a long day at work and start reading volume 1? That's what I thought. Just because a book is true and complete doesn't mean that I automatically have any interest in it.

Consider another example. On any given weekend morning, how many people set their alarm clocks early, get themselves and their children dressed, and head off to a lecture on the literature of Shakespeare, Homer, or Aristotle? Yet for two thousand years Christians by the millions have assembled under sometimes very difficult and dangerous circumstances to listen to the teachings of the Bible. Why is that? Because the words of the Bible are *alive.*

The writer of Hebrews describes the Bible this way: "For the word of God is living and active and sharper than any two-edged sword, and piercing as far as the division of soul and spirit, of both joints and marrow, and able to judge the thoughts and intentions of the heart" (4:12). The word translated "active" means "to be full of energy." The Bible is not dead and dormant; it is alive and active. In the words of one commentator, "The word of God is always doing something to those who hear or read it." Jesus made a similar claim when He said, "[T]he words that I have spoken to you are spirit and are *life*" (John 6:63).

The fact that the Bible is God's perfect, complete, and living revelation means that it is the primary means through which we hear the Master's voice. Don't be tempted to treat the Bible like a piece of third-class mail addressed to Occupant. Too many Christians are tossing aside the Bible in search of "first-class" personal revelation and are being deceived in the process.

What the Bible Won't Do

While it's important to understand the Bible for what it is, it's equally important to recognize what the Bible *is not.* Some Christians expect the

Bible to do things it was never designed to do, at times with disastrous results. For example, an automobile is a wonderful mode of transportation. However, the driver who attempts to use a car to cross the Atlantic or to fly off a steep cliff is going to be severely disappointed.

Similarly, we need to use the Bible properly, recognizing its limitations. We should not expect it to predict our future, answer all of our questions, or provide specific direction for every decision we face.

The Bible Won't Predict Our Future

Haddon Robinson relates the true story of a well-known Christian leader facing the impending death of his wife. One morning before he left home to visit his wife in a hospital intensive care unit, he noticed a promise box on the kitchen table. He reached in and pulled out a card on which John 11:25 was printed: "I am the resurrection and the life; he who believes in Me shall live even if he dies."

Overwhelmed by the promise of the verse, he reached for another card. It read, "I shall not die, but live, [a]nd declare the works of the LORD" (Psalm 118:17, NKJV). The husband was convinced that God had spoken to him. He raced to the hospital confident that God would heal his wife. In fact, he told the nurses what God had revealed to him, saying they were about to witness a miracle.

The next morning his wife died. Not only was this Christian leader devastated, but the name of God was dishonored among the hospital staff. The nurses and everyone else who had heard the husband's testimony concluded that either (a) he was a religious fanatic or (b) God was incapable of fulfilling His promise.

The truth is that neither option was correct. This man was simply guilty of using the Bible in a way it never was designed to be used. Although the Bible reveals general truths about our destiny (our death, our judgment, and our eternal home), it is not a divine horoscope that can be used to decipher specific details of the future.[3]

The Bible Won't Answer All of Our Questions

As a pastor, the questions I am asked most frequently begin with the three-letter word *why*. Why did God allow my husband to leave me? Why did God allow my child to be murdered? Why does God allow my ungodly boss to prosper? Why doesn't God answer my prayer? Why did God choose to save me instead of the Hindus in India?

The questions are endless—and ultimately unanswerable. The person who attempts to use the Bible as an encyclopedia of theological truth is going to be disappointed, since many of our deepest questions simply aren't answered.

Remember the story of Job? Here was a man who had lost everything—his possessions, his family, and his health. Naturally, Job wanted an answer to the "why" question. "Why have you allowed one of your servants to suffer like this?" Job insisted on knowing. "If this is how you treat your friends, I shudder to think how you treat your enemies." Finally, God answered Job's question—sort of—with these words:

> Who is this that darkens counsel
> By words without knowledge?
> Now gird up your loins like a man,
> And I will ask you, and you instruct Me!
> Where were you when I laid the foundation of the earth!
> Tell Me, if you have understanding,
> Who set its measurements, since you know?
> Or who stretched the line on it?
> On what were its bases sunk?

> Or who laid its cornerstone,
> When the morning stars sang together,
> And all the sons of God shouted for joy? (Job 38:2-7)

For the next several chapters God answers Job's why questions by saying, in essence, "Since I'm God and you're a mere human, there is no possible way you could understand what I am up to. Trust Me. I know what I'm doing." And Job did just that in his answer to the Lord:

> I know that Thou canst do all things,
> And that no purpose of Thine can be thwarted.
> "Who is this that hides counsel without knowledge?"
> Therefore I have declared that which I did not understand,
> Things too wonderful for me, which I did not know. (Job 42:2-3)

It's futile to try to use the Bible to answer all of life's why questions. God's ways are not our ways; His thoughts are far beyond our own.

Although it has been fourteen years since my mom was taken prematurely in death, I still don't understand why. But the Bible does provide me with an answer to the "who" question. God, through His Word, reminded me that night that He was in charge. He had a plan that He was working out, even though in the darkness I couldn't see what that plan was.

The Bible Won't Provide Specific Direction for Every Decision

I love the way the late Paul Little illustrated the misuse of the Bible in trying to hear the Master's voice. A severely depressed man was searching for direction. He hoped God would speak to him, so he opened his Bible and placed his finger on a verse: "Judas went out and hanged himself." This was not the message he wanted to hear, so he tried again. This time his finger fell on the verse, "Go thou and do likewise." That shook him up terribly, so out of desperation he tried once last time, only to read "And what thou doest, do quickly."[4]

Some Christians expect the Bible to give specific direction on the details of future life choices. For example, the Bible does not reveal the name of the person one is supposed to marry (unless that person's name happens to be Paul or Grace). You can search the Scriptures and never find specific guidance on the vocation you should pursue. A church like mine, facing the building of a new sanctuary or even a possible relocation, will have difficulty using the Bible to provide specific answers. While one group uses the story of Solomon's building of the temple to inspire faith, another group uses Solomon's admonitions in Proverbs to warn against debt. The specific answer we're looking for simply isn't there.

WHAT'S THE BIBLE GOOD FOR?

Now that we've explored three big things the Bible *won't* do for you, you might be wondering what the Bible is good for. Well, I'm glad you asked. While there are numerous benefits of studying the Bible, I'll mention just three: The Bible confirms the reality of God's sovereignty, it convicts us of sin, and it communicates God's purposes for our lives.

The Bible Confirms God's Sovereignty

Most Christians (myself included) operate in life as "practical atheists." We make plans, indulge our desires, and try to navigate through our difficulties as if God didn't exist. If you read the book of Ecclesiastes you'll find that Solomon did the same thing. That's why he spent the first eleven chapters of his spiritual journal describing "life under the sun." Apart from God, Solomon discovered that pleasure was futile, wisdom was vain, work was meaningless, government was corrupt, life was unfair, and death awaited us all. Pretty depressing, wouldn't you say?

But in the final chapter, Solomon looked at life "above the sun": "Remember also your Creator in the days of your youth, before the evil days come and the years draw near when you will say, 'I have no delight in them'" (Ecclesiastes 12:1).

Solomon told us that the only way to make sense out of life is to continually remind ourselves of God. Remember that He is there, that He loves us dearly, and that He has a plan for us that He formulated before each of us was born. Remember that there is nothing that can thwart His plans for our lives.

Dawson Trotman, the founder of The Navigators, drowned while trying to rescue two girls who had been thrown from a speedboat at Schroon Lake, New York. A friend who was with him ran to the shoreline to find Dawson's wife, Lila. "Lila, Dawson's gone!" the friend screamed. Lila calmly quoted Psalm 115:3: "Our God is in the heavens; He does whatever He pleases."[5]

That is the supernatural power of God's Word. When we are engulfed in a fog of pain and disappointment, the Bible lifts our thinking above the clouds and reveals a God who is watching, protecting, and executing His perfect plan for our lives.

The Bible Convicts Us of Sin

I can't count the number of times I've been confronted by someone, either in person or by letter, who has said, "You obviously were preaching to me today. How did you know about my situation?" Obviously I didn't, but God did. As I noted earlier, God's Word is not only living and active, but it also is "sharper than any two-edged sword, and piercing as far as the division of soul and spirit, of both joints and marrow, and able to judge the thoughts and intentions of the heart" (Hebrews 4:12).

Someone has described the convicting power of God's Word this way: The Bible is alive, it speaks to me. It has feet, it runs after me. It has hands, it lays hold of me.

The Bible Communicates God's Purpose for Us

The Bible may not provide a specific answer for every dilemma, but it *does* reveal God's will for your life. It accomplishes that by reminding you of God's bigger purpose for your life. And what is that purpose? Paul summarizes it in Romans 8: "For whom He foreknew, He also predestined to become conformed to the image of His Son, that He might be the first-born among many brethren" (v. 29).

God's overriding purpose for your life is to mold you into the image of His Son. God wants you to love what Jesus loved, think like Jesus thought, and behave like Jesus would behave in every situation. If this seems too vague, think about the ways we are guided in life by older, more experienced mentors.

Mark Foley is a friend of mine who serves as president of the University of Mobile. Prior to assuming the presidency of this Christian university, Mark served as a vice president at New Orleans Baptist Theological Seminary. During those years, seminary president Landrum Leavell taught Mark the ins and outs of the world of academia. When Mark later arrived at the University of Mobile and found himself face to face with a problem, he would simply ask himself, "What would Dr. Leavell do in this situation?" Although some of the problems were unique to Mark's institution, he nevertheless knew his mentor so well that he had no doubt what he would do if faced with a similar problem.

When our mate angers us with an unfair accusation, when our e-mail displays an advertisement from a pornographic site, or when a colleague tempts us with a dishonest business deal, Romans 8:29 encourages us to ask a simple question: "What would Jesus do in this situation?" Most of the time, the answer is obvious.

Beyond a general purpose for our lives, the Bible also communicates very specific precepts for our lives. We are to marry only another Christian (2 Corinthians 6:14). We are not to divorce except in cases of adultery or desertion (Matthew 19:9; 1 Corinthians 7:10-17). We are to pray continually (1 Thessalonians 5:17). We are to refrain from critical speech (James 3:5-12). We are to attend church regularly (Hebrews 10:24-25). We are to perform our job with enthusiasm and excellence (Colossians 3:23). We are to refrain from grumbling (Philippians 2:14). We are to share the gospel with unbelievers (Matthew 28:19-20). We are to submit to those in authority (Ephesians 5:22–6:8).

How to Hear God

Now that we've looked at God's general will for our lives, it's time to get down to specifics. If I want to hear God speak to me through His Word, what do I need to do? Let's focus on a few essentials for hearing God through His Word.

Don't Neglect Spiritual Preparation

Contrary to what many believe, God doesn't speak to everyone through the Bible. I've heard people say, "I just don't understand the Bible" and "It's so boring, I don't get anything out of it." There are good reasons for such comments. To hear God speak through the Bible you need both supernatural power and a submissive mind.

Regarding supernatural power, D. L. Moody once said, "Trying to read the Bible without the illumination of the Holy Spirit is like trying to read a sundial by moonlight." Before you can hope to understand the Bible, you need a teacher who will "guide you into all the truth" (John 16:13). That teacher's name is the Holy Spirit, and He is available only to those who have trusted in Christ as their Savior.

But being a Christian alone does not guarantee that you will understand the Bible. You also need a submissive mind. My friend and mentor Howard Hendricks often comments, "God did not give us the Bible to make us smarter sinners!" The only reason God speaks to us is so that we might obey His voice. And only when we approach the Bible with that resolve of unconditional obedience can we expect to hear the Master's voice. The psalmist saw the relationship between obedience and understanding when he vowed, "Teach me, O LORD, the way of Thy statutes, [a]nd I shall observe it to the end" (Psalm 119:33).

John Ortberg illustrates the relationship between obedience and understanding with this story from his past:

> Guidance only makes sense for people who are resolved to respond. Responding begins, of course, with obedience to God's clear guidance from Scripture. One of my college friends had been sexually involved with his girlfriend for two years. As we neared graduation, he wondered about marriage. "Is it God's will for me to marry this girl?" he asked.
>
> My friend didn't really want guidance. He already had clear scriptural guidance about sexual behavior that he wasn't the least bit interested in. He just wanted to know if this girl was the Big Deal of the Day or if he should wait to see what's behind Door No. 2.[6]

John's story illustrates one of the most basic truths about hearing the Master's voice: "Light obeyed bringeth light; light rejected bringeth night." God only speaks to those who have a submissive mind.

Develop a Plan

Imagine a person who wistfully says, "I sure would like to write a book someday." What are the chances that such a wish ever will become a reality? Slim to none. For that person to realize his dream, it will take a plan: determining a topic, developing a proposal, contacting publishers, securing a contract, writing the book, and so on. Books don't happen without a plan. And neither does anything else that is worthwhile.

A number of years ago I toured the Billy Graham Center for Evangelism in Wheaton, Illinois. Displayed in one of the glass cases was a Bible that had been given to Albert Einstein. The giver of the Bible had written a note to Einstein on the flyleaf that read: "Straws on the surface flow, but he who would search for pearls must dive below." To receive the priceless insights from God's Word demands a plan and a dogged determination to follow that plan, even for someone as intellectually gifted as Einstein.

Specifically, your plan for reading God's Word should include a period, a place, and a program.

When I say you need a *period,* I mean there should be a specific time every day that you devote to meditating on God's Word. For some of you, the early morning might be the best time. Others do better at night after the dinner dishes are put away and the children are in bed. Still others find that lunchtime provides an excellent opportunity to spend a few moments listening to God.

In his book *Point Man,* Steve Farrar confesses that for a period of time he was a "spiritual anorexic." He was starving to death spiritually because of his lack of nourishment from the Bible. Just as an anorexic has a psychological aversion to eating, a spiritual anorexic has an aversion to reading the Bible. Steve says that he was on the verge of spiritual death when he made a commitment to begin every morning by reading from God's Word. Before retrieving the morning newspaper or tuning in to the morning news programs, he would ask God to speak to him through His Word. And he says that simple decision revolutionized his spiritual life.

Are you so desperate to hear from God that you are willing to make a similar commitment?

The second requirement, a *place,* is equally important. God met Jacob at Bethel. He spoke to Moses on Mount Sinai (among other locations). And He revealed Himself to Paul on the road to Damascus. In each of these instances, God communicated to His servants in a specific geographical location. Without overspiritualizing this point, I would suggest that part of your plan for listening to God through His Word should include a specific location. Your place might be your den or sewing room or a quiet location outdoors. For me, it's a comfortable chair and ottoman in our bedroom. Next to my chair is a small electric fan I can turn on to drown out other sounds in the house to help me concentrate on listening to God.

The third requirement is a *program.* One reason some Christians derive so little benefit from the Bible is that they don't treat it with the same respect they would any other book. Imagine sitting down in your favorite chair to begin reading the novel that a friend has recommended. You open to the middle of the book and read a few paragraphs. You are immediately confronted with unfamiliar names. You then turn to the last chapter and discover that the plot is hopelessly convoluted. You then flip through the rest of the book to see if anything catches your eye. Nope, nothing there. So you close the book and check out the *TV Guide.*

No serious student would try to read a book that way, so why do we think it will work with the Bible? If you expect to hear God speak through His Word, you need to have a program for doing so. Some people advocate reading the Bible through in a year (though I often wonder why people feel like they need to race through the Bible in a year when it took fifteen hundred years to write). Another plan involves reading five psalms and one chapter of Proverbs a day for each day of the month.

I've adopted a program for reading God's Word that I learned from John MacArthur. He describes it as a method that made the Bible "come alive" for him:

> I began in 1 John. One day I sat down and read all five chapters straight through. It took me 20 minutes. Reading one book straight through was terrific. (The books of the Bible weren't written as an assortment of good little individual verses. They were written with flow and context.)
>
> The next day, I sat down and read 1 John straight through again. The third day, I sat down and read 1 John straight through.... I did this for 30 days. Do you know what happened at the end of 30 days? I knew what was in 1 John.
>
> Someone says to you, "Where in the Bible does it talk about confessing our sins?" You see a mental image of 1 John, first chapter, right-hand column, half-way down (depending on your Bible). "Where does it say to love not the world?" Second chapter, right-hand column, half-way down. "Where does it talk about sin unto death?" Chapter 5 last page. You know 1 John![7]

For longer New Testament books, such as the Gospels or Revelation, MacArthur suggests dividing them into thirds. The first month he reads the first third of the book repeatedly, the second month the second third, and the third month the final third. This approach works for MacArthur, and it might work equally well for you. It really doesn't matter what program you use, just as long as you have one.

Distinguish Between Principles and Precepts

Recently a parishioner asked a very perceptive question at our annual "Stump the Pastor" question-and-answer session: "Why is it that we Christians accept the prohibition against homosexuality in Leviticus 18, but reject the prohibition against wearing clothing made of two different fabrics in Leviticus 19?" That's a great question and one that can be answered only by understanding the difference between precepts and principles. *Precepts* are God's specific commands that apply to me. *Principles* are general truths that can be applied to my specific situation.

Here's how Chuck Swindoll contrasts precepts and principles:

> Precepts are clearly marked statements like "Abstain from sexual immorality." That's like saying "Speed Limit 35." What is speeding? Anything over thirty-five miles an hour. That's a precept.
>
> Then there are principles in Scripture, and these are general guidelines that require discernment and maturity if we are to grasp them.... [They are] like the sign that says "Drive Carefully." This may mean forty miles an hour on a clear, uncongested highway, or it may mean ten miles an hour on an ice-covered curve.... There is no sign large enough to list all the options you have when you're behind the wheel. So you must know the rules of the road, follow the signs that are there, and use all your skill combined with discernment.[8]

Here is a general guide to distinguishing between precepts (specific commands) and principles (general truths that can be applied to specific situations). The Old Testament contains principles that we can apply to our life. For example, although we are not prohibited from wearing a shirt made of polyester and cotton, there is a general principle in Leviticus 19 that applies today. As people of faith, we are to live holy and separate lives from unbelievers. We must take that Old Testament principle and ask God to reveal how it applies to our individual situation today.

However, the New Testament contains the specific commands (precepts) that govern our daily lives. It's no accident that all of the clearly revealed commands of God that I mentioned earlier (don't marry an unbeliever, pray continually, and refrain from critical speech) come from the New Testament. The apostle Paul said that all Scripture is "God-breathed" and is profitable for our lives...as long as we use it properly.

As you finish this chapter and perhaps move on to some other activity, I hope there is one truth that you will carry with you: Although God speaks in many ways, the clearest and most reliable way He communicates is through His written Word. The Bible is not static; it is dynamic. It is not dead; it is alive. It is not passive; it is active.

Oswald Chambers wrote, "The mere reading of the Word of God has power to communicate the life of God to us mentally, morally, and spiritually. God makes the words of the Bible a sacrament, i.e. the means whereby we partake of his life, it is one of His secret doors for the communication of His life to us."[9]

May I encourage you right now to close this book, find a special place where you can be alone with God, and open His Word with this prayer in your heart: "Open my eyes, that I may behold [w]onderful things from Thy law" (Psalm 119:18).

4

Our Amazing Listening God

Five minutes a day that will revolutionize your life

Dan Rather once asked Mother Teresa, "What do you say to God when you pray?" Mother Teresa answered quietly, "I listen." Surprised by her answer, Rather asked the inevitable follow-up question, "Well, then, what does God say?" Mother Teresa smiled and replied, "He listens."[1]

Have you ever considered how phenomenal it is that the Creator of the universe is actually interested in listening to *you?* The president of your company may not know your name, much less have time to listen to your concerns. Your mate may be too preoccupied with work or family concerns to give you his or her undivided attention. Your children may be so hypnotized by the computer or television that they can only manage an occasional grunt when you try to engage them in conversation. But God is there...and He is always ready to listen. Eugene Peterson wrote:

> We live in a noisy world. We are yelled at, promoted, called. Everyone has an urgent message for us. We are surrounded with noise: telephone, radio, television, stereo. Messages are amplified deafeningly. The world is a mob in which everyone is talking at once and no one is willing or able to listen.

> But God listens. He not only speaks to us, he listens to us. His listening to us is an even greater marvel than his speaking to us. It is rare to find anyone who listens carefully and thoroughly...where our minds are taken seriously. When it happens we know that what we say and feel are immensely important. We acquire dignity. We never know how well we think or speak until we find someone who listens to us.[2]

But not only does God listen when we speak, He also speaks when we listen. Do you remember God's promise to Jeremiah? A little background might help.

Jeremiah had been prophesying that his country of Judah was about to be leveled by the Babylonians because of Judah's disobedience to God. Some of the nation's leaders blasted Jeremiah's message as "politically incorrect" and threw the prophet into prison.

Understandably, Jeremiah needed reassurance that God was in control of the nation in general and of his life in particular. That's the background of the promise so many believers have claimed through the years: "Call to Me, and I will answer you, and I will tell you great and mighty things, which you do not know" (Jeremiah 33:3). When we pour out our hearts to God, we can know there is someone on the other end of the line who not only promises to listen, but also promises to answer.

An army major arrived at his new post and was excited about having his own office and a personal secretary for the first time in his career. The secretary buzzed him for his first appointment, a private. Wanting to appear far more important than he was, the major picked up the telephone and pretended to be involved in a conversation when the private entered.

"Yes, general. We enjoyed having you and the missis over for dinner last night as well. We're looking forward to next week, also. Thank you, general."

The major placed the phone in its cradle, looked at the awe-struck private and said, "Now what do *you* want?"

The private stammered, "Well, sir, I just came to hook up your phone!"

Unfortunately, many of us view prayer as simply a one-way conversation. We speak; God listens (hopefully). But God reassured Jeremiah that prayer is more than a monologue, it's a dialogue with the Creator of the universe. Henry Blackaby writes:

> Your personal prayer life may primarily be one-way communication—you talking to God. Prayer is more than that. Prayer includes listening as well. In fact, what God says in prayer is far more important than what you say.[3]

Thus, when we talk about hearing God's voice, we need to understand that one of the primary ways God speaks to us is through prayer: We speak, God listens; God speaks, we listen.

Now I must admit at the outset that I have many unanswered questions about prayer. Let me share a few of them with you. Why do we need to pray if God has already determined what is going to happen? Is a sovereign God really going to limit His actions because of the prayers—or the lack of prayers—of His people? How does God pick and choose which of my prayers He is going to answer? Why does God answer some requests that I mention only once and deny other requests that I agonize over for months? How can I know whether my request is "according to God's will"? If God does speak through prayer, *how* does He speak?

Before you get your hopes up, I should tell you that I won't be able to answer all of these questions—not because of a lack of space, but because of a lack of understanding. I don't pretend to know all the answers, and I'm suspicious of anyone who claims he does.

Still, our lack of understanding about prayer shouldn't keep us from praying. Few of us can explain in detail how an invisible force called electricity travels through miles of wire and into our homes to provide the power needed to operate our appliances. But does that lack of understanding keep us from appropriating the power that's available? I've been traveling on airplanes since I was six months old, but I can't comprehend how those big birds weighing hundreds of thousands of pounds ever get off the ground. Yet I still get on board and trust them to deliver me safely to my destination.

I have developed the same attitude about prayer. Even though I can't begin to answer all of my own questions about the subject, I still believe that prayer is a primary channel through which we hear the Master's voice. C. S. Lewis once observed that God could have selected any method He wanted to accomplish His purpose on earth, but He chose to do it mostly in response to the prayers of His people.[4]

THE DIVINE INSTRUCTOR

Most of my questions about prayer melt away when I look at the life of Christ. Jesus didn't try to explain how prayer works, He just did it. Prayer was the foundation of His earthly life and ministry. It's no surprise, then, that the disciples asked Him to teach them how to pray (Luke 11:1). These guys weren't Rhodes scholars (just think about Peter), but they were smart enough to see that prayer was the key to the supernatural power in Jesus' life. And they wanted that same power in their lives.

What was it that impressed them so much about Jesus' prayer life? As one writer asks, were the disciples curious about some special prayer language that Jesus used? No record of that. Did Jesus pray in complicated theological terms that they desired to learn? No, His prayers were actually quite simple. Were Jesus' prayers accompanied by dramatic physical gestures or supernatural phenomena? We don't find that in Scripture either. So what made such an impression on them?

I believe the disciples were impressed by Jesus' dedication to the *discipline* of praying. He didn't limit His praying to times of convenience or crisis. Instead, Jesus modeled what He preached to His disciples: "[T]hat at all times they ought to pray and not to lose heart" (Luke 18:1).

Through the years I've taken a few trips with one of my spiritual mentors, Dr. Howard Hendricks. There are two qualities about "Prof" Hendricks that have impressed me. One is his devotion to studying God's Word. Many years ago, Prof was speaking at a conference center. Late one night after he had gone to bed, I wandered into the conference room and saw his Bible lying on the lectern. As I picked it up and thumbed through it (sorry, Prof, I have never confessed to this invasion of your privacy before) I saw that just about every word in that New Testament was underlined and every page contained copious notes in all shades of ink. I understood that night that one of the secrets of Dr. Hendricks's power was his discipline in studying the Word.

But the other discipline I have observed is his dedication to prayer. It never mattered how late he went to bed or how early he had to arise, he always set the alarm clock an hour early just to spend time in prayer. That kind of dedication has taught me more about prayer than a dozen books on the subject.

I believe the disciples were similarly impressed by Jesus' example. They were like most of us who might be moved to pray if the crisis is severe enough. As pastor Bill Hybels observes, most of us are motivated to pray "when the phone call comes in the middle of the night, when your boss warns you that your job is up for grabs, when the doctor says it doesn't look good, or when your mate says someone else is starting to look good."[5]

But it didn't take a crisis to motivate Christ to speak with His heavenly Father. Jesus prayed at all times. Whether He was tired or rested, hungry or satisfied, restless or content, concerned or at peace, Jesus prayed.

Mark 1 records one of the single busiest days of Jesus' earthly ministry. He spent the entire day preaching God's truth, casting out demons, and healing the sick. I imagine that when that grueling day finally came to a close, He dropped into bed and fell asleep immediately. But even more remarkable than what happened that day is what happened the *next* day. Mark tells us, "And in the early morning, while it was still dark, He arose and went out and departed to a lonely place, and was praying there (v. 35).

Had I been Jesus I could've offered all sorts of excuses for hitting the snooze button when my alarm sounded at 4:30 A.M. "God, didn't I do enough for You yesterday? Isn't it more important that I be rested so I can be effective in my work for You? Can't I talk to You just as easily later in the day?"

Being fully human as well as fully divine, Jesus suffered the same physical limitations we suffer. He experienced hunger, thirst, sore throats, and exhaustion. That morning every muscle in His fatigued body must have pleaded with Him to stay in bed just a little while longer. But for Jesus, time spent talking with God was a priority. And I believe it was that deep commitment to prayer that made an indelible impression on His disciples. Again, these guys may not have been the brightest lights in the galaxy, but they got the point. If prayer is that important for Jesus, the perfect Son of God, how much more vital must prayer be for sinful people like us?

Why did Jesus place such a premium on prayer? Why should it be a top priority with us? As I said at the beginning of this chapter, prayer is a two-way conversation: our talking with God and God's talking with us. There are a multitude of books on prayer that offer helpful insights about speaking to God: confessing our sins, praising the attributes of God, interceding on behalf of others, petitioning God for our needs. But the focus of this book is not on *speaking* to God, but *listening* to God. The Lord has promised to do more than simply listen to us; He promises to speak to us when we pray.

What God Tells Us

If prayer is a process of listening to God, what exactly does He communicate to us? I can think of three crucial areas of guidance that come to us through prayer: God's direction, His peace, and His desires.

God's Direction

Seeking God's direction is important not just because it helps us avoid costly mistakes. To formulate our plans and execute our decisions without asking God for guidance is the essence of ungodliness. Psalm 14:4 asks, "Will evildoers never learn—those who devour my people as men eat bread and who do not call on the LORD?" (NIV). Jim Cymbala observes that God defines the wicked person as one who does not call on the name of the Lord. He lives his life without any thought of what God might desire for him.[6] I believe it is that same thought that James had in mind when he warned:

> Come now, you who say, "Today or tomorrow, we shall go to such and such a city, and spend a year there and engage in business and make a profit." Yet you do not know what your life will be like tomorrow. You are just a vapor that appears for a little while and then vanishes away. Instead, you ought to say, "If the Lord wills, we shall live and also do this or that." But as it is, you boast in your arrogance; all such boasting is evil. (James 4:13-16)

James is not condemning long-range planning or goal-setting, but he is warning about forging ahead in our plans without any consideration of God's will. Failing to consult God invites disaster. Remember the story of Israel's defeat at Gibeon? Intoxicated by their military successes over the cities of Jericho and Ai, God's people assumed they would have no difficulty destroying the evil inhabitants of Gibeon, as God had commanded them to do.

But the Israelites underestimated their opponents. The Gibeonites tricked the Israelites into making a peace treaty with them, and the Israelites had to suffer the consequences of the ill-advised covenant. What was the cause of the embarrassing debacle? The Bible tells us: "So the men of Israel took some of their provisions, *and did not ask for the counsel of the Lord*" (Joshua 9:14).

Their sin was failing to ask God for guidance—guidance that He was more than willing to provide. It's the kind of direction that James wrote about when he promised, "But if any of you lacks wisdom, let him ask of God, who gives to all men generously and without reproach, and it will be given to him" (James 1:5).

Some years ago I thought about writing a book entitled *Ten Decisions You Never Need to Pray About.* The book would have explained that some decisions don't require prayer because either (a) God already has revealed His will in the Bible or (b) the decision is a matter of personal preference. As I've said, a Christian obviously doesn't need to pray about whether he should marry an unbeliever, be faithful to his mate, or engage in a dishonest business deal. God already has spoken about those matters.

Similarly, we rarely seek God's guidance about whether to order steak or chicken for lunch, wear a blue outfit or a black one, or drive a Ford or Chevrolet. Those are matters of personal preference. Some would say that *every* decision that is not clearly addressed in the Bible is a matter of personal preference, such as the choice of a vocation or a mate. However, we saw in chapter 2 that God does in fact have a plan for our lives that includes such specific details as these. Those who oppose the idea that God has specific plans for every area of our lives would argue, "Why do you pray about the choice of a mate if you don't pray about what to have for lunch?"

James gives us the answer. "If any of you lacks wisdom, let him ask of God." According to James, we should pray for guidance about those issues that require additional insight. I mentioned in a previous chapter that we are making plans to install an image-magnification system in our church auditorium. Our staff and deacons have felt that such a system will enhance the worship services. Although the congregation embraces the idea, one naysayer approached me and said, "Why haven't you called the church to a time of prayer about this issue? How do we know whether this is God's will?"

The simple answer is "God's Word and common sense." I know that God wants people to worship effectively together. So using better technology to enhance worship is a no-brainer.

But there are plenty of other issues I face every day for which I desperately feel the need for guidance. Should I add this particular individual to the church staff? Which doctor should I choose for a second opinion? What school should I select for my child? What should I do to mend this broken relationship? Since none of the answers to these questions is clearly spelled out in Scripture, what am I to do? James advises me to pray.

They say confession is good for the soul, so here is mine to you. Too often prayer is my last resort instead of my first response. When faced with a difficult decision, my first impulse is to grab the phone and call trusted advisors or whip out my legal pad and list the pros and cons of various courses of action rather than asking God for wisdom. Do you find yourself doing the same thing? The late Paul Little wrote about his own experience:

> At the Urbana Convention in 1948, Dr. Norton Sterret asked, "How many of you who are concerned about the will of God spend five minutes a day asking him to show you his will?" It was as if somebody had grabbed me by the throat. At that time I was an undergraduate, concerned about what I should do when I graduated from the university. I was running around campus—going to this meeting,

> reading that book, trying to find somebody's little formula—1, 2, 3, 4 and a bell rings—and I was frustrated out of my mind trying to figure out the will of God. I was doing everything but getting into the presence of God and asking him to show me.
>
> May I ask you the same question: Do you spend even five minutes a day specifically asking God to show you? All of us as Christians would do well to take this question to heart. Praying for God's will is a daily responsibility, and one for which the serious Christian must make time.[7]

How does God answer when we ask Him for guidance? Sometimes it's through a unique insight that the Holy Spirit reveals in Scripture. Or it might be a timely word spoken by a friend. Or it may be that God closes a door through which we were about to enter and opens another door of opportunity. Or God might answer us through an unmistakable impulse that could only be His voice. Please don't miss the point. Our responsibility is to *ask* for guidance. His responsibility—and promise—is to *answer*.

God's Peace

Someone has defined worry as "a thin stream of fear trickling through the mind. If encouraged, it cuts a channel into which all other thoughts are drained." Most of us can identify with that observation. Have you ever found yourself totally engaged in a task at work or enjoying a diversion like a good book or television program, when suddenly, out of nowhere, a particular fear pops into your mind? Such a fear usually begins with the words *what if.* What if my mate... What if my boss... What if my job... What if my child... What if my investments...

You try to dismiss the thought, but the fear keeps returning until you can't concentrate on anything else. Worry divides our minds and drains our energy. As Corrie ten Boom once observed, "Worry doesn't empty tomorrow of its sorrow; it empties today of its strength."

The apostle Paul had plenty to worry about as he sat in prison. While he was in chains, his enemies were busy slandering his reputation. The church he founded was being invaded by false teachers. On top of all that, he was awaiting the verdict in his trial that would determine whether he would live or die. And yet, in spite of all this uncertainty, Paul wrote to the Philippians: "Be anxious for nothing, but in everything by prayer and supplication with thanksgiving let your requests be made known to God" (4:6).

What should you do when fear grips you by the throat and won't let go? Pray. I like the way the *New Living Translation* words this verse: "Don't worry about anything; instead, pray about everything." I once heard pastor David Jeremiah encourage his audience to make two lists. At the top of one list write the word *worry* and at the top of the other list write *prayer*. Use the worry list to write down all the things you are anxious about (you can use a second and third sheet if necessary). When you're done writing, you'll notice that your worry list is full and your prayer list is virtually empty. So, following Paul's example, transfer the items from the worry list to the prayer list.

What is the result of an empty worry list and a full prayer list? Paul tells us, "And the peace of God, which surpasses all comprehension, shall guard your hearts and your minds in Christ Jesus" (Philippians 4:7).

The word translated *guard* is a military term that refers to a solider standing watch at his post. The Christians in Philippi were used to seeing Roman soldiers standing guard throughout their city. Paul was all too familiar with Roman guards as well, since he was chained to a different one every eight hours. As Paul dictated the words of this letter to his secretary, he must have looked at that stone-faced Roman soldier charged with watching over him when he added the words about God's peace standing guard over our hearts and minds, protecting us from the unwelcome intruder of worry.

What are you worrying about right now? What thoughts are sapping your energy and enthusiasm? Your children? Your job? An illness? A crushing financial obligation? A broken relationship? I encourage you to create a worry list by writing down those concerns that are robbing you of joy. Once you have written all of them down, pick up your pen and transfer each item to your prayer list. As you write down each one, cross it off your worry list.

Once your worry list is empty and your prayer list is complete, close this book and spend ten minutes praying about the items on your list. As you pray, don't be surprised if you sense someone watching over you and protecting your heart and mind from worry.

God's Desires

Certainly God promises to give us direction about the things that are on *our* minds. But don't be surprised if God occasionally wants to speak with you about something on *His* mind! Consider the story of Abraham.

Abraham's early experience with God, recorded in Genesis 12–16, was nothing short of thrilling: a sudden move to a foreign country, a war with the kings of the East, four appearances by God, a night of forbidden pleasure with a slave girl, and the birth of a son. From Genesis 18 until the end of Abraham's life, things become even more eventful with the destruction of Sodom and Gomorrah, the near death of a child, a family wedding, and the loss of a mate. But sandwiched between Genesis 16 and 18 is Genesis 17 (isn't that a brilliant theological observation?). What happens in Genesis 17? Not much of anything—at least at first glance. But a further examination of this passage reveals why God designated Abraham as His "friend."

Now when Abram was ninety-nine years old, the LORD appeared to Abram and said to him,

> "I am God Almighty;
> Walk before Me, and be blameless.
> And I will establish My covenant between Me and you,
> And I will multiply you exceedingly." (Genesis 17:1-2)

Let's face it. There's nothing particularly thrilling about walking. In fact, it can become quite monotonous. You put one foot in front of the other; then you do it all over again and again. Walking might get you where you're going, but it seems to take forever. Bicycle riders, teenagers on inline skates, joggers, even children on scooters leave you in the dust. But if you develop the habit of regularly getting out and walking at the right pace, it will do wonders for your health.

The same thing could be said about walking with God. There's nothing glamorous about it. It really doesn't compare with driving down the coast in a flashy sports car. It doesn't bring the same exhilaration as racing down a Rocky Mountain ski run. Walking with God involves putting the right foot forward, and then doing it again, and then repeating the process. It lacks the adrenaline rush of miraculous healings, speaking in tongues, and other dramatic supernatural phenomena. But if you develop the habit of faithfully walking with God—every day and at a steady pace—it will do wonders for your spiritual health.

What does it mean to walk with God? Above all, it means to listen to God. At least that is how Abraham understood things. Immediately after God's command, the Bible says that "Abram fell on his face, and God talked with him" (Genesis 17:3). Abram did not fall on his face and begin talking to God. Instead, he bowed before God in complete silence and listened to His voice.

When is there time in your daily schedule to allow God to speak to you? I'm not talking about reading the Bible, as important as that is. I'm not even referring to talking with God about your concerns. When do you kneel in complete silence before God and ask Him to speak to you about the issues *He* is concerned about?

When you listen to God's voice, let me suggest three specific things to listen for:

Sins to be abandoned. Is there anything in your life that is displeasing to God? King David prayed,

> Search me, O God, and know my heart;
> Try me and know my anxious thoughts;
> And see if there be any hurtful way in me,
> And lead me in the everlasting way. (Psalm 139:23-24)

When you ask God to shine the searchlight of His Holy Spirit into the dark recesses of your heart, you can expect Him to reveal painfully specific areas of your life that need to change.

Relationships to be mended. Have you ever been trying to pray or read the Scriptures when the image of a person with whom you have had a conflict pops into your mind? I used to think of such intrusions as satanic or at least carnal. *God doesn't want anything to interrupt my time with Him*, I would rationalize. Yet in Matthew 5, Jesus says that those interruptions can originate with God:

> If therefore you are presenting your offering at the altar, and there remember that your brother has something against you, leave your offering there before the altar, and go your way; first be reconciled to your brother, and then come and present your offering. (vv. 23-24)

The Bible teaches that a clear conscience is essential, not optional, in the Christian life (see 1 Timothy 1:19). Someone has defined a clear conscience as the ability to look anyone in the eye and know there is no wrong you have not attempted to make right. The apostle Paul claims that ability is just as vital as the quality of faith in our walk with God.

Therefore, don't be surprised if while you are praying, God brings to mind the name of someone whom you have wronged and with whom you need to be reconciled. This issue of reconciliation is such a priority that Jesus advises you to drop whatever you are doing—including worshiping God—in order to mend that broken relationship.

Commands to be obeyed. As we saw in the last chapter, God did not give us the Bible to make us smarter sinners. In Psalm 119:34 David prayed, "Give me understanding, that I might impress my Bible study class with my knowledge." Just checking to see if you were still with me. No, this is what David actually prayed: "Give me understanding, that I may observe Thy law." The purpose of all divine revelation, whether it's from the Bible or prayer, is obedience.

In Abraham's case, God gave a very specific command to follow: the circumcision of himself and his descendants. Without going into great detail, this was not a particularly pleasant command to obey, especially in the days before anesthetics. Nevertheless, Abraham obeyed God completely and immediately: "*In the very same day* Abraham was circumcised, and Ishmael his son. And all the men of his household...were circumcised with him" (Genesis 17:26-27).

Thoreau once said, "It takes two to speak the truth. One to speak and another to listen." Yes, prayer is speaking to God while He listens, but prayer also involves listening to God as He communicates His direction for the issues we face, His peace for the turmoil we encounter, and His desires for the kind of life we live.

Direction, peace, and desires. At the heart of these three concepts is a single word that captures the essence of what God communicates to us in prayer: sovereignty. Prayer is submitting ourselves to the sovereignty of God in our lives. Since this book is not a theological treatise, let me give a simple definition of the sovereignty of God: "God is in control." Nothing takes Him by surprise. Nothing thwarts His ultimate purpose. Everything is under His rule. Thus, when we pray, we are saying, "God, I know You have an opinion about this issue I'm facing, and that's why I need Your direction." Or "God, I know You are in control in the midst of this crisis; that's why I need Your peace." Or "God, I know You have a purpose for my life; that's why I need to know Your desires."

As Gordon MacDonald writes, "Worship and intercession are far more the business of aligning myself with God's purposes than asking Him to align with mine."[8]

Several years ago we took a tour group to Israel and saw all the popular sights. But the most memorable experience for many of us was praying alone in the garden called Gethsemane. We knelt before our heavenly Father just as Jesus did so many years ago.

Jesus' experience that night is one giant theological conundrum to me. The Bible teaches that Jesus the Son and God the Father are one. Yet on the night before His crucifixion a battle was raging between two wills: the will of God the Father and the will of Jesus the Son. I don't understand that, and neither can you. But I do understand that Jesus didn't want to suffer the physical—and more important, spiritual—pain He was about to experience. That is why He confessed to His disciples that night in the garden: "My soul is deeply grieved, to the point of death; remain here and keep watch with Me" (Matthew 26:38).

If you have ever had difficulty obeying what you know to be God's will for your life, you aren't alone. Jesus experienced that same conflict, and He was transparently honest with God about His struggle: "My Father, if it is possible, let this cup pass from Me" (Matthew 26:39).

When you share with God your deepest feelings, remember that you aren't telling Him something He doesn't already know. Jesus was honest about His lack of desire to go to Calvary. But the next phrase in His prayer tells the whole story: "yet not as I will, but as Thou wilt" (Matthew 26:39).

Jesus wasn't praying for a revelation of God's will. He already knew what God desired. Instead, Jesus was praying for the *willingness* to do God's will. And on that night two thousand years ago, the two wills became one.

Haddon Robinson offers an interesting insight into Jesus' experience in the garden:

> In the life of Jesus, prayer was the work, and ministry was the prize. For me prayer serves as preparation for the battle, but for Jesus, it was the battle itself. Having prayed, He went about His ministry as an honor student might go to receive a reward, or as a marathon runner, having run the race, might accept the gold medal.
>
> Where was it that Jesus sweat great drops of blood? Not in Pilate's Hall, nor on His way to Golgotha. It was in the Garden of Gethsemane. There He "offered up prayers and petitions with loud cries and tears to the one who could save him from death" (Hebrews 5:7, NIV). Had I been there and witnessed that struggle, I would have worried about the future. "If He is so broken up when all He is doing is praying," I might have said, "what will He do when He faces a real crisis? Why can't He approach this ordeal with the calm confidence of His three sleeping friends?"
>
> Yet, when the test came, Jesus walked to the cross with courage, and His three friends fell apart and fell away.[9]

Prayer is ultimately aligning your will with God's will, your desires with His desires. And when you submit yourself to God's sovereign plan, you'll experience His supernatural peace.

Last year I had the opportunity to visit with pastor Ron Mehl, a writer I have long admired. For many years Ron has battled with a life-threatening disease, and yet from talking with him you'd never guess he was standing on the threshold of eternity. His conversation overflows with gratitude and inexplicable peace. What's his secret? Ron writes:

> Many people ask me how I've dealt with years of leukemia—years of hanging by a rope over the edge of a cliff. My answer might be that it's not so bad when you know who is holding the rope! I've settled into a sense of confidence that my time is in the Lord's hands. Please hear me on this: my life really is His responsibility. Because of that, I don't worry, because He's going to care for everything. Scripture says, "You can throw the whole weight of your anxieties upon him, for you are his personal concern" (1 Peter 5:7, Phillips). When you put Him first, and He's everything to you, that's what you've done.
>
> He is responsible for my life. He is responsible for the outcome. He is responsible for how long I live and how long I get to serve and minister. The weight of it is off my shoulders. He's responsible for what happens in the end—and I'm not! I just to get to enjoy the journey.
>
> In fact, I believe it is what you don't surrender that ends up eating you alive, because you carry it and feel so responsible to somehow bring it all to a good conclusion—when deep in your heart you know you never can.[10]

"Not my will, but Your will, Lord." When we utter those words, we can expect God to communicate His direction, desires, and most important, His peace to us.

A Listening Plan That Works

Up to this point you probably have agreed with everything I've said about prayer. Most Christians would. Allow me now to ask you a very personal question that I've had to ask myself while writing this chapter: Why don't you pray more? If the Sovereign Ruler of the universe has promised to communicate His direction, desires, and peace to you, why do you spend so little time listening to Him? I think pastor and writer John Piper may have an answer:

> Unless I'm badly mistaken, one of the main reasons so many of God's children don't have a significant prayer life is not so much that we don't want to, but that we don't plan to. If you want to take a four-week vacation, you don't just get up one summer morning and say, "Hey, let's go today!" You won't have anything ready. You won't know where to go. Nothing has been planned.
>
> But that is how many of us treat prayer. We get up day after day and realize that significant times of prayer should be a part of our life, but nothing's ever ready. We don't know where to go. Nothing has been planned. No time. No place. No procedure. And we know that the opposite of planning is not a wonderful flow of deep, spontaneous experiences in prayer. The opposite of planning is the rut. If you don't plan a vacation you will probably stay home and watch TV. The natural, unplanned flow of spiritual life sinks to the lowest ebb of vitality. There is a race to be run and a fight to be fought. If you want renewal in your life of prayer, you must plan to see it.[11]

Using Piper's words, let me suggest three ingredients of a successful plan for listening to God: a period, a place, and a pad. (Some of these are similar to the plan for reading God's Word that we saw in the last chapter.)

A Period

Paul tells us in 1 Thessalonians 5:17 to "pray without ceasing." The apostle says prayer should be as natural and frequent in our life as breathing. Time spent stuck in traffic or waiting in line or performing the mundane tasks of life can be redeemed by conversing with God: "Thank you, Lord, for the gift of life. Give me wisdom in what I should say next. I praise You for this unique opportunity. Please help me hold my tongue."

But there also needs to be a special time we set aside to listen to God. For Jesus, early mornings worked well (see Mark 1:35). But if you're like me and are neither sanctified nor fully conscious before 7 A.M. and two cups of coffee, then another time of the day might work better for you. It's not important when that time is on your daily calendar, but that you have one.

A Place

Recently my wife and I took our daughters back to our hometown for a high school reunion. As we approached the school, we passed a park that had been a spiritual sanctuary for me during high school. Almost every morning I'd come to that park at 7:30 A.M. (I was more spiritual back then), find a bench, and spend time with God. As we drove by that park I could remember some very definite insights God communicated to me more than twenty-five years ago, including my choice of a mate and His desire for my ministry. Over the years my place for meeting God has changed, but the principle remains the same: We all need to set aside a special place where we can meet with God.

Jesus modeled the importance of having a quiet place to meet alone with God. Before He began His public ministry, Jesus went into the wilderness to spend forty days with God. Mark tells us that Jesus went to a lonely place and prayed after the busiest recorded day of His ministry. During the greatest trial of His life, He selected a secluded garden where He could be alone with His Father.

And Jesus tells us to do the same. Allow me to paraphrase His instructions in Matthew 6:6: "But you, when you pray, go to your special place. Shut your door. Turn off the telephone, CD player, and radio, and pray to your Father in secret, and He will reward you openly."

A Pad

In recent years I've become more convinced that nothing can enhance a prayer life more than a pen and a pad of paper. Recording your requests and God's answers will not only encourage specificity in your prayers, but it will bolster your faith as you look back and see how God has answered your requests through the years.

Equally beneficial is recording what God is saying to you in your time with Him. If you've ever supervised employees (or children for that matter), you've probably experienced the frustration of having to repeat instructions to an inattentive subordinate. But when a person makes the effort to write down your wishes, you know he is serious about following your commands.

Recording the insights God communicates to us through His Word, circumstances, or impressions demonstrates that we are serious about listening. Some people call this journaling. A spiritual journal is not a diary that records what we do; it is a record of what God is doing in our lives.

Author and poet Luci Shaw recounts what drove her to start keeping a spiritual journal:

> All my life long I've thought I should keep a journal. But I never did until a few years ago, when the discovery that my husband Harold had cancer suddenly plunged us into the middle of an intense learning experience, facing things we'd never faced before. Confronted with agonizing decisions, we would cry out to the Lord, "Where are you in the middle of this?" It suddenly occurred to me that unless I

> made a record of what was going on, I would forget. The events, details, and people of those painful days could easily become a blur. So I started to write it all down.[12]

It is far too easy for the important lessons God has taught us through the years to become a blur. That's why a pen and a pad can be valuable tools for listening to the Master's voice.

We've covered a lot of ground in this chapter. We examined the priority of prayer in Jesus' life. We discussed three ways God communicates to us in prayer. And we suggested some essentials for an effective prayer plan. Unfortunately, it's possible to be in agreement with everything you've just read and still not hear the Master's voice. God exists, and He is speaking. The question is this: Are you making time to listen?

5

Signs, Circumstances, and the Will of God

Why putting out the fleece may leave you all wet

When it comes to hearing God speak, reading the Bible and praying are highly overrated activities—or so it seems. Quit looking at me that way. You've probably had the same heretical thought at times.

Let's say you're facing a major decision that will affect your family for years to come. The importance of making the right choice motivates you to sequester yourself with your Bible to hear from God. However, faithfully searching the Scriptures provides no concrete answers to your dilemma, so you resort to Plan B: prayer.

For twenty minutes every morning over the next month you pour out your heart to God. You desperately desire to know His will. While talking with your heavenly Father about your situation eases your anxiety level momentarily, you arise from your knees as perplexed as ever. There is no voice from heaven thundering, "Go ahead and accept the job offer!" You have difficulty distinguishing between the inner leading of God's Spirit and your natural desires. So what's a Christian to do?

Why not ask God for a sign? After all, doesn't the Bible say, "[I]f any of you lacks wisdom, let him ask of God" (James 1:5)? What could be more logical—and biblical—than asking God for a miraculous revelation about His will for your life?

I used the same line of reasoning a number of years ago, with disappointing results. While I was serving on the staff of a large church, I was contacted by the pastor of a similar-size church to see if I'd be interested in serving as his number-two man. The change would mean an increase in responsibility and a higher salary. And it would move me closer to fulfilling my call as a pastor (or so I thought). I was becoming increasingly restless in my present situation and was invigorated by the thought of a new challenge.

After my initial interview with the pastor and a tour of his church, he phoned me to say that everything was looking positive and he would be in contact with me soon. But the days turned into weeks, and finally several months had elapsed without any word.

One Monday I was sitting through a particularly depressing staff meeting in the church where I was serving. My prayer was "Lord, you know how miserable I am in my present condition. I really would like to move, but I need some clear direction from You. If I'm supposed to go to this church, please have Dr. _____ call me today."

When the meeting finally concluded, I walked back to my office and saw a slip of paper in my message slot. "Dr. _____ called and would like you to call ASAP," it read.

I dialed his number and after a few pleasantries heard him say, "Robert, I really don't know why I called today, but I just felt impressed to touch base and say that everything is still looking good. I'm working with the personnel committee and will be back in contact soon." Who could have asked for a clearer confirmation from God?

Now, as Paul Harvey is fond of saying, for the rest of the story. Several weeks later the pastor called me again as he had promised—but not with the news I expected. "Robert, I'm sorry, but it doesn't look like it would be best for you to come. There are internal problems in the church, and I'm not sure I have the support of the congregation. It would be unfair to ask you to come into this volatile environment." The pastor left the church not long afterward.

I was devastated, not just because I was forced to remain in my present situation a while longer, but because I felt I'd been betrayed by God. What sort of cruel trick was this? I had genuinely sought His will about serving in *His* kingdom. When I sincerely thanked God for that phone call a few weeks earlier, was He snickering in heaven over my excitement? Could I ever trust Him again?

This experience motivated me to reexamine the matter of seeking God's guidance through signs and circumstances. Does God ever provide guidance through supernatural signs? If so, what are the principles we should follow in utilizing signs and special revelation?

Supernatural Signs in the Bible

At first glance, my desire for a supernatural sign appeared to be thoroughly biblical. After all, isn't the Bible filled with stories of the miraculous signs God provided His servants who sincerely wanted to discern His will? Let's look at four of the most frequently cited instances of supernatural guidance in the Scriptures.

Eliezer and Rebekah

Long after Abraham had received his AARP card, he began thinking about his mortality and the pressing need to leave the earth populated with plenty of grandchildren. For that to occur, though, Abraham's son Isaac needed a suitable wife. Unfortunately, the land of Canaan where Abraham and company were residing was filled with ungodly Canaanite women. So Abraham dispatched his faithful servant Eliezer to return to Abraham's homeland and find a bride for Isaac.

Eliezer journeyed to the city of Nahor in search of the perfect wife for his master's son. However, the servant soon discovered that Nahor was the happening place for SFNs (single female Nahorites). He was overwhelmed by the number of potential mates for Isaac. How could he ever hope to select the right one?

Then he had an idea. Why not ask God for a miraculous sign?

> Behold, I am standing by the spring, and the daughters of the men of the city are coming out to draw water; now may it be that the girl to whom I say, "Please let down your jar so that I may drink," and who answers, "Drink, and I will water your camels also";—may she be the one whom Thou hast appointed for Thy servant Isaac; and by this I shall know that Thou hast shown lovingkindness to my master. (Genesis 24:13-14)

God apparently heard Eliezer's request and answered with lightning speed.

> And it came about before he had finished speaking, that behold, Rebekah who was born to Bethuel the son of Milcah, the wife of Abraham's brother Nahor, came out with her jar on her shoulder.... Then the servant ran to meet her, and said, "Please let me drink a little water from your jar." And she said, "Drink, my lord"; and she quickly lowered her jar to her hand, and gave him a drink. Now when she had finished giving him a drink, she said, "I will draw also for your camels until they have finished drinking." So she quickly emptied her jar into the trough, and ran back to the well to draw, and she drew for all his camels. (Genesis 24:15,17-20)

Here is a clear case of God's answering someone's request for divine guidance through a supernatural sign. But let's not stop here. There are other instances in the Bible.

Gideon and the Fleece

It's more than likely that you're familiar with the phrase "putting out the fleece" in reference to seeking a sign. If you're confused about a choice that's confronting you, ask God for a sign. "Lord, if you want me to start giving more to the church, then have my boss give me a raise tomorrow."

This idea of fleeces comes from the story of Gideon recorded in Judges 6. God had commanded Gideon to take a small army and defeat the powerful Midianites. Before embarking upon what could have been a suicide mission, Gideon understandably wanted to make sure this really was God who was speaking to him and not the tacos he had eaten the night before. So he asked God for a sign:

> "If Thou wilt deliver Israel through me, as Thou hast spoken, behold, I will put a fleece of wool on the threshing floor. If there is dew on the fleece only, and it is dry on all the ground, then I will know that Thou wilt deliver Israel through me, as Thou hast spoken." And it was so. When he arose early the next morning and squeezed the fleece, he drained the dew from the fleece, a bowl full of water. (Judges 6:36-38)

But Gideon was not overly anxious to rush into battle against the Midianites, so he asked for *another* sign.

> Then Gideon said to God, "Do not let Thine anger burn against me that I may speak once more; please let me make a test once more with the fleece, let it now be dry only on the fleece, and let there be

> dew on all the ground." And God did so that night; for it was dry only on the fleece, and dew was on all the ground. (Judges 6:39-40)

Gideon asked God for a sign to confirm His will, and God supernaturally answered his request not once, but twice.

The Apostles and the Lots

Those who would say that such supernatural signs are limited to the Old Testament and therefore have no relevance for today are obviously unfamiliar with the New Testament. A supernatural sign determined the outcome of the first decision the apostles were forced to make after the ascension of Christ.

After the defection and death of Judas, the apostles needed to select his replacement. Two nominations were made from the floor: Justus and Matthias. Since both men were equally qualified, how could the apostles discern God's will in the matter? You guessed it.

> And they prayed, and said, "Thou, Lord, who knowest the hearts of all men, show which one of these two Thou hast chosen to occupy this ministry and apostleship from which Judas turned aside to go to his own place." And they drew lots for them, and the lot fell to Matthias; and he was numbered with the eleven apostles. (Acts 1:24-26)

The practice of drawing lots was similar to the idea of rolling dice or drawing straws to make a decision. In this instance, the name of each candidate was written on a stone and place in an urn. The name that rolled out of the urn first was assumed to be God's choice.

Paul and the Man from Macedonia

Again, some theologians might say, "Each of the above instances occurred before the Holy Spirit was given to every believer. Now that God's Spirit indwells each Christian, there is no longer any need to resort to supernatural signs for guidance." That would be a wonderful argument—if it weren't for Acts 16.

For his second missionary journey, Paul planned to take the gospel message to Ephesus and Bithynia, but God had a different idea. Every attempt Paul and his companions made to enter these cities was met with a slammed door. When they finally arrived at the seaport of Troas, they were perplexed. "Should we try again to visit Ephesus, or should we go home and credit our failure to God's sovereign plan?" they wondered.

We don't know how long Paul and his cohorts stayed in Troas debating their options. But in the middle of one of those nights, God settled the issue for them with a supernatural sign.

> And a vision appeared to Paul in the night: a certain man of Macedonia was standing and appealing to him, and saying, "Come over to Macedonia and help us." And when he had seen the vision, immediately we sought to go into Macedonia, concluding that God had called us to preach the gospel to them. (Acts 16:9-10)

This was no "still small voice" that impressed Paul to change his strategy. Instead, the apostle saw a vision that clearly communicated God's will.

If Scripture so clearly teaches that God spoke time and again through supernatural signs, is it wrong to assume He would communicate in the same way to us? I confess that I come from a theological tradition that appears to limit God's options in manifesting Himself. "Now that the Bible is complete, there is no need for supernatural guidance," I've been told. But have you discovered how God delights in breaking out of the boxes we construct for Him? He doesn't always act according to the restrictions we place on Him.

After pointing out the dangers of relying on supernatural revelation for guidance, the great Hebrew scholar Bruce Waltke admits:

> Having said that, I do believe in special revelation, and I think too many conservative scholars have no place for God's special intercession because they have no control over it. We can't force God to talk, yet sometimes He completely surprises us and talks anyway.[1]

Since God is God and we clearly aren't, why couldn't He choose to speak through signs and special circumstances today?

Six Clear Signals About Signs

In His sovereignty, God may choose to communicate to us through supernatural signs. However, we need to understand six principles that Scripture gives us about such signs. These principles apply today just as they have throughout the Bible.

1. Seeking Supernatural Signs Generally Is Condemned in Scripture

The idea of seeking to know the mind of a deity (or deities) through supernatural signs is common in many pagan religions. Some groups sought divine guidance through hepatoscopy ("reading" the liver of a sacrificed animal). Others employed astrology, fortunetelling, or communicating with the spirits of the dead. God's Word clearly forbids His people from using these methods (see Leviticus 19:26,31; Deuteronomy 18:10-12).[2] While it's true that God occasionally chose to speak through supernatural signs, it's significant that signs had their origin in pagan religions.

The episode involving Gideon and the fleece is not a demonstration of Gideon's courage, but his lack of faith (maybe that's why he isn't included in the "Hall of Faith" in Hebrews 11). God already had confirmed His will through a series of miraculous signs recounted in Judges 6 (the appearance of the Angel of the Lord and the consumption of Gideon's offering by fire). No wonder Gideon was reluctant to ask God for yet another sign.

Perhaps the harshest words about seeking signs for guidance come from the lips of Jesus. The Lord rebuked the Pharisees for demanding additional signs rather than desiring to obey the revelation they already had received:

> Then some of the scribes and Pharisees answered Him, saying, "Teacher, we want to see a sign from You." But He answered and said to them, "An evil and adulterous generation craves for a sign; and yet no sign shall be given to it but the sign of Jonah the prophet." (Matthew 12:38-39)

Translation: "Why do you want any more information? You guys already know everything about Me that you need to know." Isn't the same true of us? Our problem is not a lack of information, but a lack of obedience. It's much easier to focus on the part of God's will that is hidden than to obey His commands that are plainly, and painfully, clear.

Why does God disparage the use of signs? First, the desire for signs is often motivated by a lack of faith. We confuse our desire for guidance with a desire to know the future (something God rarely reveals to us). For example, when I asked God for a sign about my potential move to another church, my basic motivation was curiosity. I was growing increasingly impatient in my present situation, and I wanted to know what God planned to do about it. But instead of unveiling His entire plan for our lives at one time, God desires that we learn how to walk with Him one step at a time.

Second, signs attempt to force God to act according to *our* terms and timetable. "If you have Sally call me by four o'clock this afternoon, then I'll ask her to marry me." But what if God isn't ready to reveal His choice of your mate by four o'clock? Or what if God indeed wants you to propose to Sally but not until some other events transpire? By issuing God an ultimatum, you're attempting to limit His choices. That's a prime reason why God is less than enthusiastic about signs.

2. Signs in the Bible Truly Were Supernatural

Often we already have a good idea of what we want to do in a given situation, so we ask for a sign that has a high probability of coming to pass. Haddon Robinson writes about a young woman who put out such a fleece:

> She told me she was thinking of going skiing, but she was seeking the mind of God as to whether or not she ought to go. I asked her how she expected to determine God's will on the matter. Very matter of factly she said, "Well, I put out a fleece. If my daddy sends me some money, then I'll know that skiing is something God wants me to do."
>
> I thought for a moment, and asked her, "Does your father send you money very often?" "Oh yes," she said, "about three or four times a year. I haven't asked him for any money lately, and I figure if he sends me money I'll know God wants me to go skiing." I appreciated her faith and her willingness to submit even the mundane decisions of her life to the guidance of God. But I thought she was undervaluing Gideon's experiences with the fleece.
>
> "Look," I asked her, "if you're really going to put out a fleece, why not a good one? After all, if you go skiing and you're not in God's will, you might break your neck. Why don't you pray that the president will send you a letter, and in that letter there will be a check

> that will give you enough to go skiing? And if you're really going to follow Gideon's example to the limit, pray that you get a second letter and a check from Britain's prime minister the next day. When you get both checks, back-to-back, you can be assured that God wants you to go skiing. That's the type of miraculous sign that Gideon wanted from God. His odds weren't 70-30; he was asking for two miracles, and he got them both!"[3]

In light of Gideon's experiences with the fleece, the sign I requested to confirm God's will about a change in churches was not that miraculous. Although I hadn't heard from the pastor in quite a while, he *had* promised to contact me. That means that every day that elapsed only increased the probability that he would call. Had I truly been seeking a supernatural sign, I should have asked for a written message in the sky (or from the president, for that matter).

3. After Pentecost, Supernatural Signs Were Given Only to Those Who Weren't Looking for Them

The last time you find God giving supernatural signs in response to a request for guidance is in Acts 1 when the apostles were trying to select Judas's successor. After that, God's supernatural revelation came unexpectedly.

Consider, for example, Paul's conversion experience. Paul (formerly Saul) was on his way to Damascus seeking to imprison believers for embracing this new heresy known as Christianity. Paul, a devout Jew, thought he was serving God by exterminating the followers of Jesus Christ. But God dramatically intervened in Paul's life:

> And it came about that as he journeyed, he was approaching Damascus, and suddenly a light from heaven flashed around him; and he fell to the ground, and heard a voice saying to him, "Saul, Saul, why

> are you persecuting Me?" And he said, "Who art Thou, Lord?" And He said, "I am Jesus whom you are persecuting, but rise, and enter the city, and it shall be told you what you must do." (Acts 9:3-6)

Was Paul seeking God's direction about whether to go to Damascus? Of course not. Nevertheless, God supernaturally revealed His will to this misguided servant.

Or think about the conversion of Cornelius. The Roman centurion was not a Christian, but he longed to know God. One afternoon an angel appeared to Cornelius and instructed him to send for the apostle Peter. Meanwhile, Peter was in the city of Joppa, and God gave him a vision as well. Peter, a conservative Jew, had trouble accepting the idea that non-Jews (Gentiles) would ever be welcomed into the kingdom of God. After all, how could God accept those who didn't follow the strict dietary laws of Judaism?

But God gave Peter a vision of animals descending from heaven. The Lord told him, "What God has cleansed, no longer consider unholy" (Acts 10:15). While Peter was reflecting on the implications of this message, the three servants Cornelius had dispatched to find Peter arrived. Again God spoke directly to Peter and told him to return with the servants and share the gospel with Cornelius.

Although Cornelius had prayed to God, he hadn't asked for a special revelation. Likewise, Peter wasn't seeking a sign from God about accepting Gentiles into the kingdom. The issue had long ago been settled in his mind. Nevertheless, God had a different idea and used supernatural signs to communicate His plan.

A third example is Paul's Macedonian vision. We already have seen how God gave Paul a supernatural vision concerning the spreading of the gospel to Greece (Acts 16:6-10). Again, there is no indication that Paul asked God for a sign, but God chose to give one anyway.

Does this mean that God absolutely won't grant anyone's request for a sign? No, but the evidence seems overwhelming that God's use of supernatural revelation is usually independent of our requests.

4. Signs Were Given as a Confirmation, Not a Contradiction, of God's Will

Kim came to my office desperate for help. "Robert, I need you to talk with my husband. He's getting ready to desert our family. I've tried reasoning with him, but he won't listen. I've asked him if he's involved with someone else, and he swears he isn't. If he leaves, it'll devastate our eight-year-old daughter."

Tony reluctantly agreed to talk with me. After thirty minutes of recounting the ups and downs of ten years of married life, he said, "I realized for the first time this week that I really never loved Kim. I got married for all the wrong reasons. As much as this is going to hurt her and our daughter, I feel like it's the right thing to do."

"How do you think God feels about your decision?" I asked. This usually is the point where the individual hangs his head in shame as if to say, "Gee, Pastor, I never thought of that before." But not Tony. In fact, I was dumbfounded by what he said next.

"I've thought about that a lot. When I first considered ending the marriage several weeks ago, I got in my car and started driving. For the next hour I drove around town praying that God would tell me what to do. Finally I said, 'God, see that traffic light up there? If you don't want me to leave Kim, turn the light red before I cross the intersection. Otherwise, I'm going through with my plan for a divorce.' The light stayed green through the intersection, and I took that as an answer."

God is not schizophrenic. He will never give you the green light to do something He has clearly prohibited in His Word. Similarly, God doesn't need to underscore an existing command by providing a supernatural sign. For example, the person who prays, "Lord, if you want me to stop this affair, show me by having my partner break up with me tonight" is out of bounds. God already has provided clear guidance on this issue. Why should He need to speak again?

While God was gracious in answering Gideon's request for two additional signs, He was under no obligation to do so. God already had commanded Gideon to attack the Midianites (see Judges 6:14). Thus, even if the fleece had remained dry, Gideon still had orders to launch the attack.

5. New Testament Signs Usually Dealt with the Proclamation of the Gospel, Not Personal Decisions

Think about God's signs to Peter, Paul, and Cornelius. Not only did these supernatural revelations come unexpectedly, but they dealt with God's priority: the spreading of the gospel.

God's vision to Paul concerned His plan to not only save Paul but also to use him as an instrument to reach the world with the good news of Jesus Christ. God's revelation to Cornelius and Peter was confirmation that God indeed was interested in Gentiles. God's supernatural vision to Paul concerning Macedonia represented a seismic shift in the apostle's missionary strategy, sending the gospel to Europe for the first time.

Interestingly, there is no record that God ever gave the apostles any special revelation about the people they were to marry, the price they should pay for a home, or what color tunics they were to wear.

6. Common Sense Usually Trumps Supernatural Signs

It's true that God occasionally asks us to do things that make no sense. God commanded Abraham to leave his family, friends, and security for an undisclosed location. God told him that he would be the father of a great nation even though he was old and his wife was barren. Finally, when God gave Abraham and Sara a son of their own, He instructed Abraham to offer that son as a burnt offering.

God continually made illogical requests of Abraham. But in each of these instances, God spoke clearly. There was none of this "I feel impressed" or "I believe God is leading me to" stuff. God's instructions were clear and precise.

If God has not chosen to give you that kind of specific revelation (and Scripture provides no clear word about your situation), I believe it makes more sense to ask for a *natural* sign rather than a *supernatural* sign. Let me explain.

Let's say you're wondering whether you should accept a certain job offer. Your mate and family feel good about the potential change, and the new job wouldn't violate any biblical principles. Furthermore, the idea of a change excites you. The only problem is that you feel the compensation you have been offered is less than it should be, and you've communicated that to your potential employer. He says he'll think about it and get back to you. So you pray, "God, if they increase their offer by five thousand dollars, I'll take this as a sign that I should accept the position."

While it appears you're being guided by signs, you're really using common sense. If your new employer is unwilling to provide a reasonable incentive for a move, does it make sense to uproot your family and risk a career change?

Garry Friesen writes that what appear to be signs are many times simply "wisdom in disguise."[4] Think about Eliezer's use of a sign to find the proper mate for Isaac. His request that the chosen bride reveal herself by her willingness to provide water for him and his camels wasn't as unreasonable as it first sounds. After all, any woman who was willing to perform such a task was obviously gracious—a wonderful quality for any potential wife. Not only that, she'd possess great physical stamina. A "dry" camel required twenty gallons of water, and Eliezer had ten of those animals. That means Rebekah had to carry two hundred gallons of water from a nearby well in order to complete the task. Such physical strength would be a necessity for the five-hundred-mile journey back to Canaan to meet her groom, Isaac. Thus Eliezer's request for guidance was based on wisdom more than on the supernatural.

Does the Master ever speak through supernatural signs? He has in the past, and on occasion He may do so in the future. But there are two much more reliable ways to discern the voice of God, as we will see in the chapters that follow.

6

Who Speaks for God?

Three people you should consult before making any major decision

"Dad, would you please help me with this math problem?"

I don't know about your house, but around our place the most reliable translation of that question is "Dad, would you please give me the answer to this problem so I can finish my homework and go online with my friends?"

I'm tempted at times to do just that. It would be much more efficient for me to solve the problem, give the answer to my daughter, and return to my more pressing commitments (like watching *Larry King Live*). Giving that kind of help would provide momentary satisfaction to both of us, but it also would short-circuit my daughter's academic development. Instead, I need to put down the remote control and help her work through the problem herself. Yes, it takes longer, but the end result is a student who develops the skills necessary to succeed in life.

I try to remember that analogy every time I get frustrated with God for refusing to give me "the answer" I feel I so desperately need.

Should I say yes to this opportunity?

Is it better for our church to relocate or stay where we are?

What should I do about this pressing financial decision?

If I were God (scary thought, isn't it?), this is how I'd reason. "I have an answer for Robert's dilemma that will best suit his life, as well as My kingdom. Since I can't be sure that he'll turn to the right section of Scripture for guidance, pray long enough to discern My voice, or even think to ask for a supernatural sign, I'll write the answer in block letters in the clouds." Doesn't that make sense?

But more important to God than our discovering "the answer" is the process by which we arrive at the answer. As we saw in chapter 2, God's overriding purpose for our lives is to mold us into the image of His Son. Above anything else, God desires to develop in us the qualities that characterized His Son: dependence upon Him, faith, love, self-control, and purity, just to name a few.

How does God encourage our spiritual development? Not by acting as a divine bellhop who is always on call to deliver what we want, when we want it. Instead, God uses trials to hammer away anything in our character that doesn't resemble Christ.

The great evangelist Vance Havner used to relate the true story of a small town in Alabama where the main industry was growing cotton. One year when it seemed that the crop would be particularly productive, boll weevils invaded and destroyed the cotton. The local economy was wiped out. However, the farmers decided that they wouldn't let boll weevils rob them of their livelihood. One man decided to raise peanuts, another planted a different crop, and the rest followed their example. Before long, the town's economy was restored, and the city became known as Enterprise, Alabama. The citizens of Enterprise even erected a monument to—you guessed it—the boll weevil. Havner concluded:

> "All things work together for good" to the Christian, even our boll weevil experiences. Sometimes we settle into a humdrum routine as

> monotonous as growing cotton year after year. Then God sends the boll weevil; He jolts us out of our groove, and we must find new ways to live. Financial reverses, great bereavement, physical infirmity, loss of position—how many have been driven to trouble to be better husbandmen and to bring forth far finer fruit from their souls! The best thing that ever happened to some of us was the coming of our "boll weevil." Without that we might still have been a "cotton sharecropper."[1]

God uses struggles to produce maturity. And that simple truth explains why discerning the Master's voice isn't always as easy as we wish it were. Reading divine messages in the sky, listening to a thundering voice from heaven, or even following a miraculous sign is effortless, but it requires no maturity. In contrast, the process of meditating on Scripture, listening to God in prayer, evaluating signs and circumstances, discovering our desires, discerning whether those desires are in alignment with God's desires, and ultimately trusting in His sovereignty produces the kind of spiritual maturity God desires in each of us.

All of which brings us to the subject of this chapter: hearing God through other people. At first glance, trusting other people to faithfully deliver God's message to you may seem like a high-risk activity. Remember the old game of Gossip in which one person whispers a message to another person who whispers it to another? When the last person in the room finally shares the message with the group it barely resembles the original communiqué.

Why would you ever trust someone else to speak for God? And if you were God, why would you trust a fallible human being to deliver your message? In human terms it doesn't make sense. Yet the Bible repeatedly encourages us to seek wise counsel when attempting to determine God's will:

The way of a fool is right in his own eyes,
But a wise man is he who listens to counsel. (Proverbs 12:15)

Through presumption comes nothing but strife,
But with those who receive counsel is wisdom. (Proverbs 13:10)

Without consultation, plans are frustrated,
But with many counselors they succeed. (Proverbs 15:22)

I'm beginning to understand why God encourages us to listen to others. If God's only goal is communicating the right answer to our questions, then relying on other people is highly inefficient. However, if God's greater purpose in our life—even greater than discovering the right answer—is to develop us into spiritually mature individuals, then it's easy to see how listening to and evaluating the counsel of others accomplishes that purpose.

Remember, there is no guaranteed recipe for discovering God's specific will for your life (two parts Bible, one part prayer, sprinkle in some good advice). Likewise, while we always should consider the counsel of others (as the above proverbs indicate), we should never expect that God will speak through every person we consult.

Nevertheless, God often uses other people to communicate His plan for our lives. And the process of weighing the counsel or obeying the commands of others produces three character qualities that God highly prizes: obedience, discernment, and dependence. Let's look at three types of people God uses to speak to us and the corresponding character qualities we are likely to develop in the process. We will see the different ways God speaks through authority figures, wise counselors, and fellow Christians.

Authority Figures

More than thirty years ago I attended the Institute in Basic Life Principles Seminar conducted by Bill Gothard. It was there I first heard the term "chain of command." The idea is that God has placed each of us under the authority of certain individuals, and it's our responsibility to obey those authority figures. Why? Because God communicates His will for our lives through those He has placed over us.

Whether that authority figure is a believer or not is irrelevant because God is in control of everyone, including unbelievers (see Proverbs 21:1). If you want to know God's desire for your life in a specific situation, seek the counsel of those in authority over you, Gothard instructed us.

The chain-of-command concept is a biblical one. With a few exceptions that I'll mention at the end of this chapter, you should always heed the *commands* and at least consider the *counsel* of those whom God has placed in leadership over you. The Bible specifically mentions five authority relationships.

Husbands and Wives

I love the story about the man who died and arrived at heaven to discover two signs above two different lines. Above one line the sign read "All Those Men Who Have Been Dominated by Their Wives, Stand Here." That line seemed to stretch through the clouds into infinity. The other sign read "All Those Men Who Have Never Been Dominated by Their Wives, Stand Here." Only one soul was standing beneath that sign.

The new guy grabbed that gentleman by the arm. "Hey, buddy, what's the secret? That other line has millions of men in it, and you're the only one standing in this line." The man looked around with a puzzled expression, shrugged his shoulders, and said, "I don't know. My wife just told me to stand here."

The truth is that wives are not to dominate their husbands—and husbands are not to dominate their wives, either. Now before you men start quoting Ephesians 5 to me, let me remind you of what the text says:

> Wives, be subject to your own husbands, as to the Lord. For the husband is the head of the wife, as Christ also is the head of the church, He Himself being the Savior of the body. But as the church is subject to Christ, so also the wives ought to be to their husbands in everything. (Ephesians 5:22-24)

Significantly, Paul doesn't use the word *obey* here as he later does in reference to slaves obeying their masters and children obeying their parents. Husbands are not to treat their wives as slaves or children, barking out orders and expecting a salute and a "Yes sir."

Instead, Paul uses the military term *hupostasso*, which means "to arrange under rank." In any organization, whether it be the military, the government, a corporation, or the church, there must be a system of authority and submission. Someone must have the final say, and in the home, the husband is the one who carries that responsibility. This doesn't mean women are inferior to men in any way. But when a woman chooses to enter into a marriage relationship, she's voluntarily placing herself under the authority of her husband.

For some of you this may be a foreign or even distasteful idea, so perhaps the analogy that Paul employs in 1 Corinthians 11:3 will help: "But I want you to understand that Christ is the head of every man, and the man is the head of a woman, and God is the head of Christ."

Did you catch that last phrase? "God is the head of Christ?" Let me ask a question. Is God the Father superior to Jesus Christ the Son? Not at all.

They are eternally coequal. But at a point in time, Jesus Christ voluntarily submitted to the will of His Father in order to accomplish the mission of salvation. In the same way, women are completely equal to their husbands, but they are called upon to submit themselves to the leadership of their husbands.

Now before some of you men transform yourselves into little Hitlers, read what Paul says to *you*:

> Husbands, love your wives, just as Christ also loved the church and gave Himself up for her; that He might sanctify her, having cleansed her by the washing of water with the word, that He might present to Himself the church in all her glory, having no spot or wrinkle or any such thing; but that she should be holy and blameless. So husbands ought also to love their own wives as their own bodies. He who loves his own wife loves himself; for no one ever hated his own flesh, but nourishes and cherishes it, just as Christ also does the church, because we are members of His body. (Ephesians 5:25-30)

Did you notice that Paul spends more time addressing husbands than he does wives? Why? Because leadership is not about privileges, it is about responsibility. If God is going to speak to a wife through her husband, then that husband must make sure he is more concerned about meeting his wife's needs than his own. Any leader who places his own privileges above the interests of those he is leading is doomed to failure.

While God does speak to wives through their husbands, the converse is true as well. Remember Pilate's wife? She advised him to "[h]ave nothing to do with that righteous Man [Jesus]" (Matthew 27:19), but Pilate refused her counsel and the result—at least from a human perspective—was disastrous.

Children and Parents

God also works through parents to communicate His will to children.

> Children, obey your parents in the Lord, for this is right. Honor your father and mother (which is the first commandment with a promise), that it may be well with you, and that you may live long on the earth. And, fathers, do not provoke your children to anger; but bring them up in the discipline and instruction of the Lord. (Ephesians 6:1-4)

When I was a youth minister, students often asked me, "How can I know what school to attend?" or "How can I know whether this is the person I should marry?" I would respond by asking, "What do your parents say?" I still remember those "What galaxy are you from?" looks I received in response. Nevertheless, God does sometimes communicate His will to children through their parents.

However, the parent-child authority structure is limited. Paul addresses this command to *children,* not to adults. As children mature, they begin to make more decisions independently. The acts of grown children moving away from home, graduating from college, and beginning their own families transform the parent's role from "authority figure" to "advisor." While adult children are under no obligation to obey their parents, they are wise to carefully evaluate the counsel of the two people who know and love them the most.

Employer and Employee

"Slaves, be obedient to those who are your masters according to the flesh, with fear and trembling, in the sincerity of your heart, as to Christ," Paul writes in Ephesians 6:5. While the slave-master relationship is not identical (hopefully) to the employee-employer structure today, God does communicate in a limited way through our bosses.

When your employer gives you a task to do, you are to perform that task enthusiastically, realizing that it's God whom you are serving (Ephesians 6:6-8). If obeying your employer's command is tantamount to obeying God, then it means that God is speaking through your employer to accomplish His purpose.

Government and Citizens

A similar relationship exists between government officials and citizens.

> Let every person be in subjection to the governing authorities. For there is no authority except from God, and those which exist are established by God. Therefore he who resists authority has opposed the ordinance of God; and they who have opposed will receive condemnation upon themselves. (Romans 13:1-2)

I had to remind myself of these verses this week when our city council ordered citizens not to water their lawns more than once a week, due to a lack of rain. Since the flowers in front of our house were starting to droop and we were preparing for a party, I considered disobeying the ordinance "for a higher purpose" (what could be more noble than a party for our deacons?). But God's Word doesn't give me that privilege. God has a plan for the well-being of our city that He executes through those He has placed in leadership.

As we'll see in a moment, there are times that we shouldn't obey government. But those exceptions don't invalidate this basic principle.

Spiritual Leaders and the Congregation

I recently had lunch with my friend and mentor Howard Hendricks and, as always, came prepared with a long list of questions. "Prof, what's the greatest issue you see confronting churches today?" Without hesitating, Hendricks answered, "Who's going to call the shots." The issue of authority has increasingly become a battleground for many congregations.

I used to think the problem of authority was one of hermeneutics. If we could accurately exegete the biblical texts, then we could answer the question of church polity. "Does the Bible teach that the pastor, congregation, or elders have the final say in the church?" But I've come to believe that the real issue is not *identifying* the true leader of the church, but *submitting* to that leadership once it is identified.

None of us likes being told what to do—especially in the church. Submission to any authority—pastor, elders, deacons, or congregations—goes against the grain of our basic nature. Nevertheless the Word of God commands:

> Obey your leaders, and submit to them; for they keep watch over your souls, as those who will give an account. Let them do this with joy and not with grief, for this would be unprofitable for you. (Hebrews 13:17)

I personally believe that Scripture teaches that the pastor is the leader (though not the only leader) in the church. He is appointed by Christ as the undershepherd to lead the congregation while the Chief Shepherd is absent (1 Peter 5:1-4). The pastor is responsible for leading the congregation in a loving, Christlike way to achieve its God-given mandate. The congregation is responsible to submit to the leadership of the pastor, who ultimately will answer to the Chief Shepherd for the well-being of the flock.

Nevertheless, the spiritual leader's authority over the congregation is limited. There is nothing in Scripture that indicates that this authority extends beyond matters directly relating to the church. Occasionally someone will come to me asking for advice about his career. "Pastor, since you're my spiritual authority, I want to know what you think I should do." I quickly pass the hot potato back to the inquirer, assuring him that my authority doesn't extend to his personal life. I can give counsel and share biblical principles, but I can't speak ex cathedra about questions not clearly answered in Scripture.

While there are several important exceptions to this principle, don't let those exceptions blur the general principle: God often communicates His will through the commands of those in leadership positions. Following those commands not only helps us discern God's individual will for our lives, but it also develops the quality of obedience that God desires in each of us. To paraphrase the words of the apostle John, "If you can't obey the leaders whom you can see, how will you ever learn to obey God whom you can't see?"

Counselors

We've seen how God speaks to us through various types of authority figures. Now we'll consider the importance of seeking wise counsel.

Haddon Robinson tells the story about a businessman who took a golf pro with him to the golf course. The businessman wanted the pro to help him improve his technique. After every swing, the pro would offer suggestions about changing the businessman's stance, the direction he looked, and his overall approach to the game. But with every suggestion came an objection. The businessman, who was a successful CEO of a major corporation, insisted that his way of swinging the club was more comfortable. Before long, the golf pro began agreeing with him.

Another golfer watched this exchange with great interest. After seeing the businessman pay the pro and the pro walk away with a giant grin on his face, the man approached the golf expert and asked, "What happened? In the middle of the session you just began to tell him what he wanted to hear." The golf pro responded, "You know, I've been at this long enough to know what people want. That man wasn't paying me for counsel; he was paying for an echo."[2]

God's Word continually encourages us to seek genuine counsel, not self-affirming echoes, when we are faced with major decisions. Why? The Bible teaches that God often communicates His wisdom through those counselors. Consider the unfortunate example of King Rehoboam.

When Rehoboam succeeded his father, Solomon, as king of Israel, the people were physically and economically "wasted" after the massive building programs from Solomon's reign. Thus, at the beginning of Rehoboam's reign, the people made an appeal to their new leader: "Your father made our yoke hard; therefore lighten the hard service of your father and his heavy yoke which he put on us, and we will serve you" (1 Kings 12:4).

Wisely, Rehoboam refused to give a quick answer and instead promised to consider their proposal for three days. He called a meeting of his father's most trusted advisors and asked for their counsel. "The people aren't exaggerating," the advisors told him. "Although your father was a great man, he pressed too hard. Give them a break as they requested, and they will follow you anywhere."

But instead of embracing their advice immediately, he sought the opinions of some of his contemporaries. "The people are testing you to see if you're a leader or a cream puff," they opined. "You've got to show them who's boss. If you give in to their first request, no telling what they'll demand next." Rehoboam concluded that these younger counselors had a better grasp of modern, tenth-century B.C. management principles than his father's advisors, so he went with their recommendation.

Rehoboam called the people together to announce his decision. "My father was a wimp compared to me. I'm going to make you work so hard that you're going to long for the days of dear old dad." You can imagine the response. The people revolted, the kingdom was torn in two, and Rehoboam was credited with a civil war that destroyed Israel.

Rehoboam's experience illustrates four principles about the importance of wise counsel when attempting to hear God's voice.

1. When faced with a difficult decision, seek advice from experts. You've probably heard the definition of an expert. Since "ex" can be defined as a "has been" and a "spurt" is a drip of water under pressure, an "expert" is a has-been drip! Nevertheless, a wise person understands that there are individuals who know more than he does about many situations. To his credit, when Rehoboam sought counsel, he first approached those people who had a long and respected track record in governmental affairs.

Some might misunderstand what I'm about to say, but I'll voice it anyway. *Usually* it's more important that the person whose advice you're seeking be knowledgeable than spiritual. For example, if you have a crack in the foundation of your home, would you call your pastor for advice? If he's anything like me, he wouldn't have a clue what to do (or even where the foundation was). If you want advice about your foundation, go to an engineer; if you want financial advice, seek out a financial planner; if you need legal advice, find the best attorney in town. If you need spiritual counsel, ask the advice of someone who walks with God.

You may be wondering, "What about the verse in Psalm 1 that describes the joy of the one who 'does not walk in the counsel of the wicked'?" (v. 1). The clear warning is against following advice that contradicts the law of the Lord. But even unbelievers can offer sound advice. For example, there's no indication that the counselors who first advised Rehoboam were particularly godly men, but nevertheless their advice was sound.

2. When faced with a difficult decision, seek advice from a variety of people. Again we need to give Rehoboam some credit for desiring a second opinion. After consulting with his father's inner circle, he sought the opinions of a completely different group. Rehoboam had learned well the lesson of his father, Solomon, who had written "Without consultation, plans are frustrated, [b]ut with *many counselors* they succeed" (Proverbs 15:22).

All of us have a tendency to seek advice from those people who will tell us what we want to hear rather than what we need to know. And like the golf pro, there are plenty of people who are willing to serve as echoes. That's why this next principle is crucial.

3. Consider the motivation of your advisors. Could it be that your financial planner is more interested in the commission he'll generate than in your financial well-being? Does your attorney have an ulterior motive in advising you to settle the case?

Had Rehoboam asked a similar question, he might have spared himself a disaster. His father's advisors had nothing to gain by suggesting that he listen to the people. They were advanced in age and realized they had no place in his new administration. The younger men, however, probably were attempting to ingratiate themselves with their friend-turned-monarch. They knew well his tendency to play BMIK (Big Man in the Kingdom), and so they tailor-made their advice to fit his corrupt personality.

4. Follow wise advice. Not all advice is to be heeded. One reason God encourages us to solicit counsel from others is so we might develop the discernment necessary to choose between good and evil, wisdom and folly.

But once we have obtained wise counsel, it's important that we follow it. Has the doctor advised you to have the operation? Then do it. Has your attorney advised you to update your will? Then do it. Has your pastor advised you to reconcile that relationship? Do it.

Unfortunately, the final epitaph of Rehoboam's reign begins with these words: "So the king did not listen." To hear good counsel and not act upon it is really not to hear at all.

Fellow Christians

There is a third human channel through whom God often speaks—one that many of us ignore. The spirit of individualism that is woven throughout our national heritage causes us to discount the importance of one of the most logical conduits of God's voice: other Christians. Henry Blackaby put his finger on this problem when he wrote:

> One of the problems many evangelical churches face today is that they have so emphasized the doctrine of the priesthood of believers they have lost their sense of corporate identity. What does that mean in simple words? Christians think they stand alone before God and that they are not accountable to anyone else, including the church.[3]

Not only are Christians accountable to one another, but we are dependent on one another. That's why the Bible's favorite metaphor for the church is the human body:

> For the body is not one member, but many. If the foot should say, "Because I am not a hand, I am not a part of the body," it is not for this reason any the less a part of the body. And if the ear should say, "Because I am not an eye, I am not a part of the body," it is not for this reason any the less a part of the body. If the whole body were an eye, where would the hearing be? If the whole were hearing, where would the sense of smell be? But now God has placed the members, each one of them, in the body, just as He desired. And if they were all

one member, where would the body be? But now there are many members, but one body. (1 Corinthians 12:14-20)

The human body is a marvelous demonstration of cooperation. Every part is dependent upon the other. For example, your stomach gets hungry. Your nose smells a hot dog nearby. Your eyes locate the hot dog vendor. Your feet transport you to the hot dog stand. Your hands douse the hot dog with mustard and shove it into your mouth, which sends it to settle your growling stomach. Now that's cooperation!

But what if your entire body were to become a giant nose? Where would you place the hot dog (your nostril perhaps?)? Or what if you were one gigantic eyeball? Although you could spot a hot dog ten miles away, you'd be helpless to do anything about it. God designed the human body in such a way that all the parts depend upon one another.

God says it's the same way in the church. No matter how self-reliant you think you are, you're incomplete without the gifts and insights other believers have to offer. We're like the two porcupines in the frozen Canadian tundra that huddled together to keep warm. They needed one another, even though they needled one other.

As we've seen in the previous section, God can use unbelievers to communicate to us. He even used a donkey to speak to the prophet Balaam (Numbers 22:27-31). But in this section, I want us to consider how God communicates through other members of His body. Fellow Christians can offer us three things we need when seeking to hear the Master's voice.

1. Insight concerning our dilemmas. I've read that occasionally when some subordinate would offer former President George Bush unsolicited advice, he'd reply, "If you're so smart, why aren't *you* president?" Most of us are naturally defensive about receiving counsel from others. Nevertheless, other individuals can offer us insight we don't possess. Consider the Exodus 18 story of Moses and his father-in-law, Jethro.

Jethro came to visit his son-in-law when Moses was the leader of the two-million strong nation of Israel. Although Jethro was proud of Moses, he was distraught by what he saw as they spent a day together on the job.

> And it came about the next day that Moses sat to judge the people, and the people stood about Moses from the morning until the evening. Now when Moses' father-in-law saw all that he was doing for the people, he said, "What is this thing that you are doing for the people? Why do you alone sit as judge and all the people stand about you from morning until evening?" (Exodus 18:13-14)

Let me paraphrase Jethro's observation: "Moses, you're out of your mind! You can't personally take care of two million people. It's not fair to them, nor is it good for you. There has to be a better way." So Jethro outlined a simple plan to relieve Moses of some unnecessary stress. He encouraged his son-in-law to spend the bulk of his time alone with God and then communicate the principles of God's Word to the people as a whole, rather than trying to counsel them individually. (This still is a relevant piece of advice for pastors today.) In addition, Jethro suggested that the people be divided into more manageable groups and that leaders be appointed over those smaller groups.

Understand that Moses didn't solicit Jethro's counsel. Nowhere does the Bible indicate that Moses was so overwhelmed by his job that he began seeking advice from management experts. He probably would have kept leading in the same way for the rest of his career. But God sent Jethro with a word of wisdom that revolutionized Moses' leadership and probably lengthened his life.

Fortunately, Moses didn't respond to Jethro's suggestion with a "If you're so smart, why didn't God make *you* the leader of Israel?" Instead, "Moses listened to his father-in-law, and did all that he had said" (Exodus 18:24).

How do you react when people offer you suggestions? Do you automatically dismiss unsolicited counsel? Do you resent it? Obviously, not everyone who volunteers advice is a messenger from God. Nevertheless, a wise person understands that occasionally God will send a Jethro to provide us with a solution to our dilemmas.

2. Guidance concerning serving God's kingdom. Imagine that over the last several months you've realized that too much of your time is consumed by the urgent rather than the eternal. You understand that your primary purpose is to advance God's kingdom rather than your own, and you've specifically asked God to reveal how best to accomplish that.

You receive a phone call from the chairman of your church's nominating committee. "We've been praying about who could best serve in ______ (you fill in the blank), and we feel God is leading us to you. Would you consider serving in this way?" How would you respond?

It would be popular in many Christian circles to discount such an occurrence. "The committee is being 'led' out of desperation, not true conviction. They're looking for someone to fill a job no one else will take." It's true that the existence of a need doesn't necessarily constitute God's call. Just because there's a shortage of missionaries in Indonesia doesn't mean that I'm supposed to go.

Nevertheless, we find a number of instances in the New Testament in which God uses a group of Christians to communicate His will to individuals, especially in matters related to service in His kingdom. For example, the decision to select Stephen, Philip, and five other men as the first deacons in the church "found approval with the whole congregation" (Acts 6:5). A group of believers approached these seven men and said, "We believe it's God's will for you to serve as deacons." The decision to send Paul and a group of men to Antioch on a specific mission was made by "the apostles and the elders, with the whole church" (Acts 15:22).

Admittedly, listening to a group of Christians who purport to know

God's will for your life is not a foolproof method for discerning His guidance. I remember a time when two search committees were talking to me about coming to pastor their churches, and both were convinced it was God's will. Obviously, someone was wrong.

The guidance we receive from other Christians needs to be evaluated by other criteria we are discovering in this book. Yet we should understand that God does speak through His church, especially when it comes to ministry opportunities.

3. Correction in our behavior. Many years ago God used a grandmother in a church I pastored to deliver a message I didn't want to hear. "Robert, if you don't deal with this issue, it will destroy your ministry." Initially I was infuriated. "Who does she think she is, trying to come in here and run my life? After all, I'm a minister 'called by God.'" But the old adage was true: The scalded dog barks loudest. I realized she was right. As a result of her rebuke, I made an extremely painful change that salvaged my life and ministry. That woman is now in heaven, but I'm eternally grateful that she had the courage to tell me what I didn't want to hear.

Do you have someone in your life like that? Is there an individual—or a group of individuals—who love you enough to warn you when you're headed in the wrong direction? And when they do, how do you respond? The Bible encourages us to carefully consider the correction (or reproof) that comes into our life:

> He is on the path of life who heeds instruction,
> But he who forsakes reproof goes astray. (Proverbs 10:17)
>
> Whoever loves discipline loves knowledge,
> But he who hates reproof is stupid. (Proverbs 12:1)
>
> A man who hardens his neck after much reproof
> Will suddenly be broken beyond remedy. (Proverbs 29:1)

A Few Warnings

We've seen the ways God guides us through the advice of authority figures, counselors, and fellow believers. Submitting to the commands of our leaders develops obedience. Considering the counsel of others requires discernment. Listening to the suggestions of other believers who may have been providentially sent to us promotes dependence on other members of the body of Christ. But as valuable as the counsel and correction of others is, it also can be misused. Whenever we receive input from others, we need to keep in mind these three cautions:

1. Don't let counsel become a cop-out. Other people's advice should never be used as a delay tactic or an escape from doing what you already know to be the right thing. Bruce Waltke writes, "It has been my experience that many Christians will go to counsel for one of two reasons: Either they aren't close to the heart of God themselves, so they are looking for a backdoor into His will, or they aren't so much looking for wise counsel as they're looking for approval from another person."[4] In my personal life and pastoral experience, I've discovered that most of the time our problem is not *discovering* the will of God, but *doing* the will of God.

2. Often, counsel is in error. Don't blindly accept the counsel of other people as a word from the Lord. Many times people are wrong. The majority of people in Noah's day were wrong when they tried to discourage him from building the ark. The majority of the spies who were sent into Canaan were wrong about the "impossibility" of taking possession of the land. All of Job's friends were wrong in their analysis of the cause of his suffering.

3. Measure all counsel against the Word of God. Any command or advice that violates the clear teaching of Scripture is to be ignored. While we are to submit to those in authority over us, that obedience has boundaries. As

Peter said when he was ordered to stop preaching the gospel, "We must obey God rather than men" (Acts 5:29).

First Kings 13 relates a tragic story about a young prophet whom God had commanded to go to Bethel, condemn a pagan altar, and return home. God clearly told him not to eat or drink, but to return home immediately after finishing his task.

But the young man was deluded by an older "prophet" who invited him to his home for a meal. The young prophet protested, "God told me to go home." But the older prophet wouldn't take no for an answer. "I also am a prophet of God, and He told me to invite you to my home for a meal." The young prophet reasoned that a "new" word from God must be more relevant than an older piece of revelation, so he accepted the old man's invitation. Listen to how this strange story ends.

> Now it came about, as they were sitting down at the table, that the word of the LORD came to the prophet [the older man] who had brought him back; and he cried to the man of God who came from Judah, saying, "Thus says the LORD, 'Because you have disobeyed the command of the LORD, and have not observed the commandment which the LORD your God commanded you, but have returned and eaten bread and drunk water in the place of which He said to you, "Eat no bread and drink no water"; your body shall not come to the grave of your fathers.' "... Now when he had gone, a lion met him on the way and killed him, and his body was thrown on the road, with the donkey standing beside it. (vv. 20-22,24)

The moral of the story? God will never contradict Himself. He won't communicate one message to you and send a different message through the advice or commands of another person. The clear commands of the Bible always trump any other means of revelation.

Up to this point we've considered two directions to which we should look when trying to hear God's voice: *upward* (prayer and Scripture) and *outward* (supernatural signs and counsel from others). In the next chapter we'll examine a third source of divine direction that rarely is discussed but is highly reliable: the look *inward.*

7

To Thine Own Self Be True

How God uses your desires to communicate His direction

"If you could choose any career or ministry, what would you choose to do? If you had all the time, education, and finances necessary and God promised that you wouldn't fail, what would you do with your life?"

Mary Cleminson immediately knew the answer as she listened to the speaker at her church's annual women's conference. "I'd be standing in your place speaking to this group!" she mused.

Mary's silent but emphatic response almost embarrassed her, but her discontent had been building for years. In college she had majored in communications. Her mentor, a successful writer and speaker, had envisioned great success for Mary. "You have a rare mix of charisma and communication skills. There is no limit to where those gifts will take you."

Apparently there was. In her senior year, Mary met and married Jonathan. For the next three years, she put her career on hold and worked as a paralegal to help put Jonathan through law school. Upon graduation, he was hired as an associate in a prestigious firm. But while Jonathan was getting invaluable work experience, his salary failed to pay all the bills, so Mary continued her work. Finally, Jonathan was granted partner status with all the accompanying financial perks. Mary quit her job and spent the next eighteen years rearing three children.

Now that her kids are in junior high and high school, she is beginning to question whether she should pursue her dream of becoming a motivational speaker. On occasion, Mary has accepted invitations to speak to civic clubs and church groups. Every time she speaks, she hears the same comments: "I've never heard anyone like you before! May I send a tape of your presentation to a friend who might want you to speak to her group? You were born to do this!"

Now that Mary's in her early forties, she knows that if she's going to pursue a career in speaking, she needs to begin now. But as a committed Christian, she wants to know whether such a career is God's will, so she sought the counsel of two trusted advisors.

Beth, a best friend since college, had been on Mary's case for years to pursue a speaking career. When Mary told her she was seriously considering it, Beth was excited and even offered to help serve as her manager.

"But Beth, how do I know if God really wants me to do this? After all, this would affect Jonathan and the kids. I want to be sure this is the right thing to do."

Beth was quick with her reply. By "divine providence" she had been reading a book on discovering God's will and had a novel concept to share with her struggling friend.

"Mary, would a speaking career in any way violate the teaching of the Bible?"

"No, I don't think so."

"Have you prayed about this decision?"

"You know that I've prayed about this for years."

"What does God say to you when you pray?"

"Well, to be honest, I don't really hear Him saying anything."

"Have you sought the counsel of other people?"

"Well, my college professor always told me I'd become a successful speaker. And whenever I speak, people are very affirming."

"All right, Mary, if you've searched the Scriptures, prayed, and sought the counsel of other people, then you're free to do whatever you want to do!"

"What do you mean?"

Beth explained what she had read about finding God's will. "One of the ways that God reveals His will to us is through our desires. After you've searched the Bible, prayed, and sought good counsel, you're free to do whatever you want. Remember the psalm that says, 'Delight yourself in the Lord and He will give you the desires of your heart'?"

At first Mary felt that Beth's advice was the green light she needed to finally fulfill her dream. But over the next few days some serious doubts began to plague her. "How can I know if my desires are from God or if they're the result of my own selfish ambition?" After struggling with her doubts, Mary called her Bible study leader, Amy, for some advice.

"Mary, what you heard from Beth sounds so good, but it is *so* wrong. You can't trust your desires. Do you have a pen and a piece of paper? I want you to write down these verses: Jeremiah 17:9: 'The heart is more deceitful than all else [a]nd is desperately sick; [w]ho can understand it?' Philippians 3:3: 'put no confidence in the flesh.' James 3:14: 'But if you have bitter jealousy and selfish ambition in your heart, do not be arrogant and so lie against the truth.'

"I don't want to hurt your feelings, but your dream of being a speaker seems to be rooted in selfish ambition. Those kinds of desires don't come from the Lord. To claim they do is to 'lie against the truth,' as James said."

Now Mary was thoroughly confused. How could two committed Christians who genuinely wanted the best for her offer such contradictory advice? Her search for God's will illustrates what appear to be conflicting teachings in the Bible concerning the value of using our desires to decipher God's will. Some, like Beth, would adopt John Calvin's famous motto: "Love God, and do as you please." Obviously, desires that violate boundaries established by Scripture, prayer, and wise counsel are off-limits. The person who decides to have an affair, declines God's supernatural call to the mission field, or decides to disobey an authority figure (for other than scriptural reasons) is acting against God's will, regardless of what his heart tells him.

Nevertheless, many of the decisions we confront aren't addressed in Scripture, can't be resolved by prayer, and become confused by conflicting counsel. Therefore, asking the question, "What does your heart tell you to do?" seems to be a reasonable way to determine God's will.

Yet Mary's Bible study leader also has a valid point. Part of the fallout from the Fall is the corruption of our desires. How does a pastor know whether his desire to erect a new building springs from his love for God or his desire for greater recognition in his denomination? How can a young man know whether his feelings for a prospective mate are rooted in sacrificial love or in ordinary lust? How can Mary know whether her dream of speaking to thousands stems from a desire to serve others or a need to satisfy her flagging self-esteem?

God's Word and Our Desires

As we look through the Scriptures, we find three important insights regarding the role of inner desires in helping us to hear the Master's voice. The Bible's view is sobering but also encouraging. Let's take a look.

1. Our desires have been corrupted by sin. Score one for Mary's Bible study leader. Sin has indeed corrupted our desires. Comedian Woody Allen, in one of his more reflective moments, said, "For all my education, accomplishments, and so-called wisdom, I can't fathom my own heart." He may not be able to comprehend the mysteries of the heart, but a man who lived two thousand years ago gave us a detailed x-ray of the human condition, and the prognosis is not encouraging. Consider Paul's words in Romans 3:10-12:

There is none righteous, not even one;
There is none who understands,
There is none who seeks for God;
All have turned aside, together they have become useless;
There is none who does good,
There is not even one.

Theologians often use these verses to support the doctrine of the "total depravity" of the human race, a doctrine that many have difficulty accepting. How can Paul say six times in three verses that there is not one righteous person on the earth and that no one does good? Just look around. The world is filled with people who love their families, volunteer at hospice, and give to the United Way. Some of those people are Christians and others aren't, but none of them appears *totally* depraved.

However, when we speak of total depravity we aren't claiming that people always act as corruptly as they could. Instead, Paul is saying that sin has corrupted every part of our lives. For example, I remember making homemade ice cream with my father when I was young. After mixing the delicious ingredients, we'd pour the mixture into the steel container and place it in a bucket containing ice and salt. During the freezing process, my father would remind me to make sure none of the rock salt accidentally got into the ice cream container. Why? Just one or two particles of salt would ruin the entire batch—something I learned the hard way on more than one occasion.

In the same way, it takes only a little sin to contaminate every part of our lives. Total depravity doesn't mean we're as bad as we could be, but it does mean we're as bad off as we could be. While some of our desires may be noble, they have nevertheless been contaminated by sin.

Now for the good news.

2. Our desires can be transformed. Corrupt desires don't have to stay corrupt. It's possible for our desires, which are naturally opposed to God's will, to be transformed into desires that align with God's will. We'll discuss the process for that transformation in the next section, but for now notice the possibility of such a transformation:

> For the mind set on the flesh is death, but the mind set on the Spirit is life and peace, because the mind set on the flesh is hostile toward God; for it does not subject itself to the law of God, for it is not even able to do so; and those who are in the flesh cannot please God. However *you are not in the flesh* but in the Spirit, if indeed the Spirit of God dwells in you. (Romans 8:6-9)

Without God's Holy Spirit controlling our lives, we can't please God. But Christians don't have to live apart from God's Spirit. Paul's words remind me of the old joke about the two men in West Texas sipping a cold drink at the local service station. "I wonder how hot it is?" one man asked. "I heard on the news that it was 110 degrees in the shade," the other answered. "Well, whatever we do, we'd better stay out of the shade!"

Paul says, "Whatever you do, stay out of the flesh! Live your life under the Spirit's control, and you'll please God."

3. God can direct us through our transformed desires. When our desires are in line with God's desires, they can serve as a reliable indicator of God's direction in our lives. Why? Because God is the originator of many of the desires we have. Consider Paul's words to the Christians at Philippi:

> So then, my beloved, just as you have always obeyed, not as in my presence only, but now much more in my absence, work out your salvation with fear and trembling; for it is God who is at work in you, both to will and to work for His good pleasure. (Philippians 2:12-13)

Some people (especially Baptists like me) get nervous around the phrase "work out your salvation." But Paul didn't say "work *for* your salvation"; he said "work *out* your salvation." The word translated "work out" refers to the working of a farm to yield the greatest harvest possible. Paul is simply saying that it takes hard work to achieve maturity in the Christian life.

There are some who adopt a passive attitude toward the Christian life. "Let go and let God" or "Quit trying to live the Christian life, and let Christ live it through you" are their battle cries. But such philosophies lead to a passive attitude that results in a life overgrown with sin. In 1 Timothy 4:7 Paul commands us to "Discipline [ourselves] for the purpose of godliness." We derive our English word *gymnasium* from the word translated *discipline (gymnaze).* You can almost smell the sweat all over this verse. It takes hard work to become a mature Christian.

Unfortunately, some Christians try to exempt themselves from that kind of hard work by making God responsible for their godliness—or lack thereof! Are you familiar with the term "upward delegation"? When a boss gives a subordinate an assignment, and the subordinate returns the assignment to the boss saying "I can't do this; you'd better do it for me," that's upward delegation. When we say, "God, it's Your responsibility to make me into a mature Christian," we're practicing upward delegation. But God refuses to accept sole responsibility for our maturity. He says, "This is an assignment I gave to you. You work it out."

I can say, "Lord I want to know Your Word better," but I'm the one who must set the alarm clock fifteen minutes early. I can pray, "Lord, help me develop a more devoted prayer life," but I'm the one who has to say no to that extra television program. I can plead with the Lord to "protect me from this temptation," but it's my feet that have to do the running, not His.

Now if that responsibility seems too heavy for you to bear alone, remember what the Bible says: "[F]or it is God who is at work in you, both to will and to work for His good pleasure" (Philippians 2:13).

As one writer points out, there really are two workers in this passage.

We are to work, but God also is working in us. I believe J. B. Phillips's translation best captures what Paul is saying here: "For it is God who is at work within you, giving you the will and the power to achieve his purpose."

The word translated *work* is *energeo,* from which we get our word *energize.* God is energizing you by giving you both the desire and the ability to accomplish His will. While salvation is a work of God alone, sanctification (becoming more like Christ) is a cooperative effort between God and me. God works in me, and I work it out. F. B. Meyer describes the relationship between God's work and our work:

> [God] may be working in you to confess to that fellow Christian that you were unkind in your speech or act. Work it out. He may be working in you to give up that line of business about which you have been doubtful lately. Give it up. He may be working in you to be sweeter in your home, and gentler in your speech. Begin. He may be working in you to alter your relationships with some with whom you have dealings that are not as they should be. Alter them. This very day let God begin to speak, and work, and will; and then work out what He works in. God will not work apart from you, but He wants to work through you.[1]

The important principle is that many times our desires come from God. He is the One who is working in us, giving us the desire to follow Him.

Desires Put to the Test

Even though God wants to transform our desires, not all of our desires originate with God. Remember Mary Cleminson? She wondered how to know whether her desire to become a speaker was a reliable indicator of God's will. There was no clear answer from Scripture, and her friends gave conflicting counsel. If you, like Mary, are questioning whether God wants you to pursue a major dream, use the following principles to lead you to an answer.

1. We need to discover our desires. To do that, you'll need to look inward. Don't spend endless hours contemplating your navel, but realize that some introspection can be healthy. In Romans 12:3 Paul advised, "I say to every man among you not to think more highly of himself than he ought to think; but to think so as to have sound judgment."

Immediately after that verse, Paul launches into a discussion of the different spiritual gifts God has given to every Christian. One key to discovering your unique spiritual gift is self-evaluation. Before you can know your gift, you have to honestly answer some questions: What am I good at? What am I not so good at? Which ministries energize me? Which ministries drain me?

Self-evaluation can also be a valuable tool in discovering God's will in other life areas. If indeed God directs us through our desires, it's important that we uncover those desires. My friend Bobb Biehl is an expert at asking penetrating questions. Here are just a few of the questions Bobb suggests for uncovering your deepest desires:

- If you could do anything you wanted, if God said you were free to choose, and you had all the time, money, staff, education, etc., you needed, and you knew for certain that you couldn't fail, what would you do?
- Where do you see yourself ten years from now?
- What causes 80 percent of your frustration, tension, and pressure? Why? What brings you 80 percent of your pleasure, joy, and fun? Why?
- What is the key to understanding the real you that most people miss?
- What have been the three biggest highlights and three biggest

hurts of your life? What are your three main hopes for your future?

- What is your life's dream? (What do you want to accomplish before you die?)
- If you could accomplish only three measurable things before you die, what three things would you accomplish?
- What three changes in yourself would most please God?
- The compliment you would most enjoy receiving would be...
- What is your single greatest strength?[2]

2. Our desires must be consistent with the Scriptures. We discussed this principle at length in chapter 5, but it's worth repeating: God will never direct you to do anything that violates His Word. No matter how strongly you might want to leave your mate, engage in a dishonest practice, or disobey any God-ordained authority, you can be *certain* that those desires don't come from God. In a contest between God's Word and personal desires, the Bible beats inner desires every time.

3. Desires should be checked by common sense. Suppose after reflecting on your dreams, you conclude that you want to quit your job and start your own business. As you thumb through the Bible, there is no prohibition against beginning a software company. But how do you know if such a desire is from God? You need to ask some basic questions: How will I provide for my family during the start-up phase? How do others in the business rate my chances for success? Do I have the necessary gifts and temperament to be successful in this kind of business? What would make my product or service unique?

Generally speaking, God is not going to ask you to do something that doesn't make sense. "Wait just a minute!" I can hear you protesting. "God often asks us to do things that make no sense. Noah building a boat in the desert didn't make sense. Abraham uprooting his family to move to an undisclosed location didn't make sense. Joshua and Caleb encouraging the people to conquer Canaan didn't make sense."

Excellent points. But notice that in each of these instances, God supernaturally and definitely revealed His will. These men had no doubt that God had spoken to them. So here's a piece of advice that's worth the price of this book: If God audibly tells you to do something—even if it violates common sense—you'd better do it! But apart from such supernatural revelation, your desires should be checked by common sense.

4. The reliability of our desires is proportionate to our spiritual health. When I go for my yearly physical, my doctor wants to be sure that I am healthy. A virus or fever can skew the results on my blood work or stress tests and render them inaccurate. In the same way, before we can trust the reliability of our desires, we need to know the condition of our heart. Godly desires don't flow out of a sick heart. Jesus said, "For the mouth speaks out of that which fills the heart. The good man out of his good treasure brings forth what is good; and the evil man out of his evil treasure brings forth what is evil" (Matthew 12:34-35). Our words reveal what's in our hearts. But that principle also applies to our desires. An ungodly heart will bring forth ungodly desires.

A number of years ago, there was a period when I was living totally apart from God. I was engaged in what many would label a successful ministry, but inwardly I was in a state of spiritual decay. I wasn't reading my Bible, praying, or living obediently. It was during that period that I began to feel a strong urge to leave the ministry and begin another career. I began to read books and consult with friends about that particular field. I dreamed of entering that new vocation, yet it was a dream that came from a heart that was desperately ill. As my spiritual life strengthened, those desires evaporated completely.

Let's go back to Philippians 2:13 for a moment. "[F]or it is God who is at work in you, both to will and to work for His good pleasure." How do God's desires become your desires? David Jeremiah reminds us that a toaster can't produce toast unless the appliance is connected to the outlet so that its Nichrome wire is heated by electricity. In the same way, we must be plugged into God's power before His desires and energy can flow through us. Specifically, there are two conductors through which God's desires and supernatural power pass into our lives. The first conductor is God's Word:

> And for this reason we also constantly thank God that when you received from us the word of God's message, you accepted it not as the word of men, but for what it really is, the word of God, which also performs its work in you who believe. (1 Thessalonians 2:13)

The second conductor that encourages the flow of God's power and desires into our lives is prayer:

> And in the same way the Spirit also helps our weakness; for we do not know how to pray as we should, but the Spirit Himself intercedes for us with groanings too deep for words; and He who searches the hearts knows what the mind of the Spirit is, because He intercedes for the saints according to the will of God. (Romans 8:26-27)

God uses His Word and prayer to transform our hearts to the point that the desires that flow into our hearts from above and the desires that flow out of our hearts become one river. Bruce Waltke writes:

> As you develop a heart for God, you find that your desires change and become consonant with the heart of God. You can find examples of this throughout Scripture. The apostle Paul regularly speaks of his desires. He tells the Romans, "I long to see you so that I may impart

> to you some spiritual gift to make you strong" (Romans 1:11). He encourages the Corinthian believers to follow their hearts: "If some unbeliever invites you to a meal and you want to go, eat whatever is put before you without raising questions of conscience" (1 Corinthians 10:27). He even shares why he has made certain career choices when he reveals "It has been my ambition to preach the gospel where Christ was not known, so that I would not be building on someone else's foundation" (Romans 15:20). Paul simply says, "This is what I wanted to do, so I did it."[3]

The more you love God, the more you can do as you please and know you are within the will of God.

5. Our desires are subject to God's sovereign plan. Sometimes our desires may correspond to Scripture, wise counsel, and common sense, but they still may be in conflict with God's plan. Consider the experience of King David, as expressed by his son Solomon:

> Now it was in the heart of my father David to build a house for the name of the LORD, the God of Israel. But the LORD said to my father David, "Because it was in your heart to build a house for My name, you did well that it was in your heart. Nevertheless you shall not build the house, but your son who shall be born to you, he shall build the house for My name." (1 Kings 8:17-19)

David was a man "after God's own heart." With the exception of a few lapses (the one with Bathsheba being the most memorable), David generally was in tune with God. Furthermore, God affirmed David's desire to build a permanent place to worship the Lord. Nevertheless, God told David that he wouldn't be the one to build the temple. God gave no reason (at least not one that is recorded here). He simply said, "I have another plan." God's decree superseded David's desire.

While knowing our desires can help us discover God's plan for our lives, there are occasions when our desires will conflict with the sovereign plan of God. In some inexplicable way, even Jesus experienced that contest of desires with His heavenly Father. In the Garden of Gethsemane, Jesus made it clear that He would prefer not to go to the cross, even though that had been the Father's plan before the beginning of time. Two very different desires collided that night. One said "go," and the other said "I don't want to go." But in the same breath that Jesus voiced His preference, He also submitted to the wishes of His Father. "Yet, not My will but Yours be done." Jesus' constant willingness to submit His will to God's will explains why His desires and God's will flowed together as one river.

It's no accident that the only time Paul ever commands us to *find* the will of God is after he has encouraged us to *submit* to the will of God:

> I urge you therefore, brethren, by the mercies of God, to present your bodies a living and holy sacrifice, acceptable to God, which is your spiritual service of worship. And do not be conformed to this world, but be transformed by the renewing of your mind, that you may prove what the will of God is, that which is good and acceptable and perfect. (Romans 12:1-2)

The only desires that truly can be trusted for direction are those that have been transformed by the power of God and placed on the altar of God.

We have looked at some of the channels through which God speaks to Christians: the Bible, prayer, supernatural revelation, the counsel of others, and our own desires. Now it's time to apply these principles to two of the biggest questions any of us will face.

Part Three

Obeying the Master's Voice

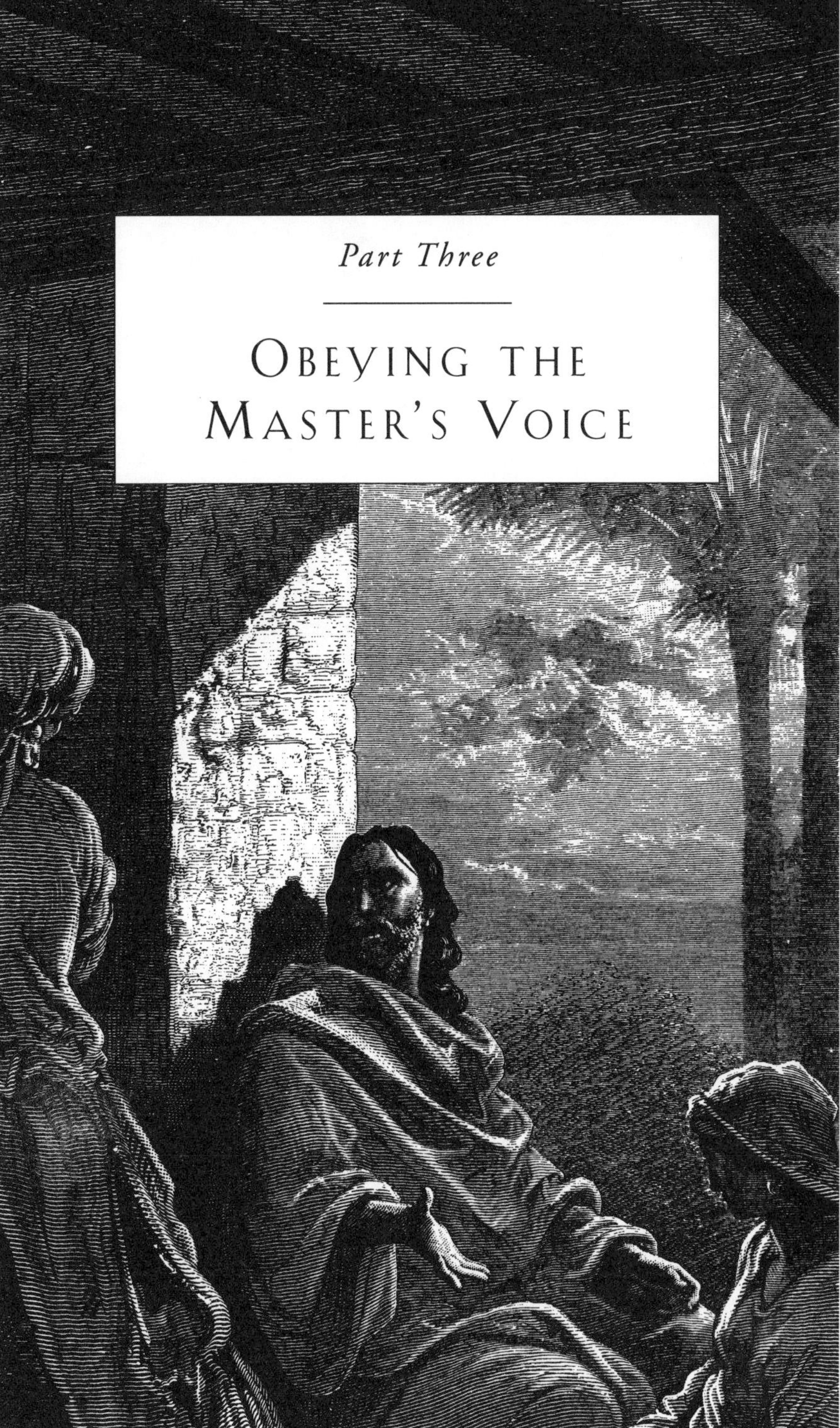

8

Marriage, Money, and the Will of God

Five principles for discovering the right mate and the perfect job

It would be a waste of time to read this book if all it did was present interesting theories about the will of God. We need to know how to apply the theory to difficult, real-life decisions. That's what we'll do in this chapter, but first let's review what we know about hearing the Master's voice.

First, we've seen that God has a personal plan for each one of us that encompasses everything from whom we marry to the types of ministries we get involved in. Is that really so hard to believe, given how interdependent the various facets of our lives are? We can be confident that God has a detailed master plan for the world in general and for our lives in particular.

Second, we can't always know God's specific plan for our lives ahead of time. Sometimes His plan can be discerned before the fact; other times it can be understood only in retrospect; and sometimes it is altogether inscrutable. Our responsibility is to listen to and obey God's voice when He does speak.

Third, God speaks in a variety of ways. When we seek His direction, we can look above (the Bible and prayer), without (counsel and circumstances), and within (our own desires). Not all of these sources carry equal weight, however. If I'm deciding whether to claim a questionable deduction on my taxes, I only need to consult one source: the Bible. Regardless of what I determine from circumstances, personal desires, or prayer, God's Word has the final say. At the other end of the spectrum, whether to wear a blue coat or a brown one is predominantly a matter of personal preference.

However, the big decisions we wrestle with require us to consider all of the means by which God speaks. In this chapter, we'll apply the principles to two of the greatest decisions we confront: the choice of a mate and the choice of a career.

Marriage and the Will of God

Last year the Fox television network attempted to capitalize on America's insatiable desire for money and sex by airing a special called "Who Wants to Marry a Multimillionaire." The show, which received blockbuster ratings, was a case study in how *not* to choose a mate. Five women agreed to be paraded before a multimillionaire, hoping they would be chosen as his life partner. Before an audience of tens of millions of viewers, the man and the lucky winner were married on camera in hopes they would live happily ever after.

Unfortunately, all did not turn out as the show's producers had hoped. According to news reports, the bride and groom stayed in separate rooms on their honeymoon and never consummated their marriage. Ultimately, the marriage was dissolved. The show's producers conceded that the show was a terrible idea (rivaled only by their previous hit "Good Pets That Go Bad") and canceled plans for future episodes.

I mention this program because it seems to resemble the story of Isaac and Rebekah in Genesis 24: A third party arranges a marriage for two individuals who have never laid eyes on one another. But fortunately, Isaac's story has a happy ending because the parties involved followed God's principles.

We looked at the background of Genesis 24 in chapter 5. Abraham, concerned about his lack of heirs, sent his servant Eliezer to find a mate for his son Isaac. Notice how Eliezer's actions illustrate the principles we've examined for hearing the Master's voice.

Principle #1: Know the *Precepts*

Before we try to discern whom to marry, we first need to discover whether God wants us to marry at all. In 1 Corinthians 7, Paul explains that marriage is not for everyone.

> Now concerning virgins I have no command of the Lord, but I give an opinion as one who by the mercy of the Lord is trustworthy. I think then that this is good in view of the present distress, that it is good for a[n unmarried] man to remain as he is.... But if you should marry, you have not sinned; and if a virgin should marry, she has not sinned. (vv. 25-26,28)

Paul goes on to explain the benefits of the single life:

- Singles suffer less in times of persecution than those who must watch their families suffer.
- Singles escape the natural friction of a marriage relationship.
- Singles can devote more energy to serving God.
- Singles don't have to share the remote control (just kidding).

How can we know if God has called us to a single life? I remember as a teenager going to hear Josh McDowell speak. He often told a tragic story about a painful breakup he had with his girlfriend. The tale would have the whole audience in tears. He then would challenge us to be open to the possibility that God may have given us the gift of singleness.

Believe me, for a group of teenagers in hormone overdrive, that was the last gift we wanted. I remember my girlfriend (now my wife) and I usually would break up for a few weeks after hearing this talk, convinced that God's will must be the most distasteful course of action we could imagine: being single. But after a few weeks our desires would carry the day, and we'd get back together.

What we didn't understand at the time was that our burning desire to be married was a key indicator that God hadn't given us the gift of being single. Paul said virtually the same thing:

> Yet I wish that all men were even as I myself am. However, each man has his own gift from God, one in this manner, and another in that.
>
> But I say to the unmarried and to widows that it is good for them if they remain even as I. But if they do not have self-control, let them marry; for it is better to marry than to burn. (1 Corinthians 7:7-9)

Here is Paul's bottom line: Marriage is God's plan for the majority of people. If you're one of those whom God has chosen for a life of singleness, you'll know it. Most of us, however, aren't questioning *whether* to marry, but *whom* to marry. And the first principle for hearing God's voice in this all-important matter is to obey God's precepts. What direction does God's Word offer us about this decision?

The primary command that regulates our selection of a mate is that believers are to marry only other believers. Authors Bill and Lynn Hybels call this "the most unpopular requirement for marriage." And yet it also is the most basic.

Abraham was living in Canaan when he asked Eliezer to find a bride for his son. The problem with Canaan, however, was that it was inhabited by ungodly Canaanites. That's why Abraham sent Eliezer back to the home country to find a wife for his son (Genesis 24:2-4). Throughout Scripture you find this principle repeated: Believers are limited to marrying only other believers. Paul commanded the Christians at Corinth, "Do not be bound together with unbelievers; for what partnership have righteousness and lawlessness, or what fellowship has light with darkness?" (2 Corinthians 6:14).

God has good reason to emphasize this command, since marriage to an unbeliever destroys our relationship with God (not positionally, but practically). Through the years, teenagers and single adults have tried to make a case for "missionary dating." "But Pastor," they plead, "by dating (or marrying) this unbeliever, I can have a positive influence on him and maybe win him to Christ." But Scripture says that influence usually works in the opposite direction. You don't pull an unbeliever up to where you are; the unbeliever will pull you down. It happened to the Israelites when they intermarried with the Canaanites, even though God had warned them against it (Deuteronomy 7:3-6). It happened to Solomon when he wed foreign wives (1 Kings 11:1-2,4). And it most likely will happen to you if you choose to marry a non-Christian.

Marriage to an unbeliever not only damages our relationship to God, but it also can fracture our relationship with our spouse. Look again at 2 Corinthians 6:14: "Do not be bound together with unbelievers; for what partnership have righteousness and lawlessness, or what fellowship has light with darkness?"

The phrase *bound together* carries the idea of two unequal animals, such as an ox and a donkey, being harnessed together to perform a task. The ox pulls against the donkey and the donkey works against the ox, resulting in constant friction and an ultimate stalemate. Believers and unbelievers are similarly mismatched, Paul says. How can righteousness and lawlessness be joined in the same harness? They are pulling in opposite directions.

And what do light and darkness have in common? They are opposites. One displaces the other. If you enter a dark room and turn on the light, the darkness disappears. Darkness and light cannot coexist.

The same truth applies in marriage. Our relationship with Jesus Christ should be the single most important aspect of our lives. So how could we develop intimacy with someone with whom we could never share that integral part of our lives? In the spiritual world, opposites don't attract, they repel!

Let me add one other word here. When looking for a mate, make sure you don't select a person who is a Christian in name only. Your life partner needs to be a growing Christian whose primary desire in life is to please God. If you were to ask me what is the number-one cause of marital conflict, after more than two decades of ministry I'd tell you: the union of two spiritually incompatible people. One spouse is sold out to following Christ; the other couldn't care less. Few marriages can survive, much less prosper, when the individuals within that marriage are pulled in opposite directions.

Proverbs 24:3 reminds us that "[b]y wisdom a house is built, [a]nd by understanding it is established." Imagine what would happen if two carpenters attempted to build a house from two different—and contradictory—sets of blueprints. One carpenter is trying to build a one-story dwelling, while the other is constructing a two-story home. One tries to pour a slab foundation, while the other uses a pier-and-beam foundation. Can you imagine the endless arguments and paralyzing frustration the two workers would experience? The final structure would be a disaster. But that's exactly what happens to couples who try to build their marriage without a common spiritual foundation.

Principle #2: Rely on *Prayer*

With a clear understanding of his master's command, Eliezer traveled to Abraham's home country. After the long journey, the servant and his camels were thirsty, so they went to the local watering hole for some refreshment. But Eliezer had another motive for going directly to the town well.

If you wanted to find some hot (literally) single women in Nahor, this was the place to go. Every evening, they came to the well to draw water for their homes (Genesis 24:11). Eliezer understood the importance of going where the village's unmarried young women would gather. But he quickly encountered the dilemma that many single adults experience: too many potential candidates! If only one woman had shown up, then discerning God's will would have been easy. But since the well attracted so many young women, what was Eliezer to do?

Those who teach that God has no specific blueprint for each person's marital future would have offered this advice to Eliezer: "Quit worrying about finding the right mate and instead concentrate on finding the right *kind* of mate. As long as you follow God's precepts (marriage only to a believer), you're free to choose whomever you want."

Does God have a plan that includes a specific mate? Eliezer thought so. Read carefully the prayer he offered when confronted with so many possibilities:

> O Lord, the God of my master Abraham, please grant me success today, and show lovingkindness to my master Abraham. Behold, I am standing by the spring, and the daughters of the men of the city are coming out to draw water; now may it be that the girl to whom I say, "Please let down your jar so that I may drink," and who answers, "Drink, and I will water your camels also";—may she be the one whom Thou hast appointed for Thy servant Isaac; and by this I shall know that Thou hast shown lovingkindness to my master. (Genesis 24:12-14)

Eliezer believed God had a precise plan for Isaac that included one specific woman who would be his bride—"the one whom Thou hast appointed." Some critics of the "one woman for one man" view claim that this case is unique because of God's one-of-a-kind promise to Abraham and his descendants recorded in Genesis 12. But obviously God's interest in people extends beyond the boundaries of ancient Israel.

Don't you imagine God had a specific plan for the marriages of the parents who would produce John Wesley or Billy Graham? And if God has designed every aspect of our being, as we see in Psalm 139, doesn't it make sense that He also arranged for the marriage of our parents? And if God directs our every step (Proverbs 16:9), isn't it reasonable to assume that He directs our steps down the aisle?

Realizing that there is one person God has selected as our mate should not drive us to panic, but to prayer. God promises to give us wisdom if we ask Him (James 1:5). He won't leave us to fend for ourselves but promises to send His Spirit to guide us (John 14:16-18). The same God who directed Eliezer will direct you.

Principle #3: Take Notice of What's *Practical*

As we saw in chapter 5, Eliezer's request for a sign from God was based on common sense. The young woman who was both willing and able to water Eliezer's ten camels had the character quality (graciousness) and physical ability (stamina) necessary to fulfill her role as Isaac's wife.

Similarly, we should use some common sense in the selection of a mate. If you're a woman who is enjoying a successful career that you want to maintain, it would be unwise to marry a man who wants you to stay home and produce babies. If you're a man who feels called to serve God in the jungles of Africa, you might think twice about marrying a woman whose idea of hardship is staying at a Holiday Inn. A person who can't be happy without several pets scurrying around the house should rethink a lifetime partnership with someone who is allergic to animals.

God asked the Israelites a penetrating question: "Can two walk together, except they be agreed?" (Amos 3:3, KJV). Such a question should not be restricted to spiritual matters but applied also to other issues about which we feel strongly. While diversity can be celebrated in marriage, we would do well to remember the words of Philip Melanchthon: "In essentials, unity. In nonessentials, liberty." You alone can determine what those essential areas of agreement must be.

Principle #4: Take Heed of Your *Preference*

"Robert, my fiancé, is a dedicated Christian. He and I agree about all the important issues. Our backgrounds are incredibly identical, and we share many of the same goals. Logically, he is a perfect guy to marry, and I should be thrilled. But I just don't feel any 'spark,' if you know what I mean. What do you think I should do?"

I have been asked this question numerous times. Early in my ministerial career I offered the conventional Christian counsel: "Romantic love is highly overrated and is peculiar to Western culture. Don't worry about the lack of a 'spark.' Just marry the right person, and the feelings will follow."

I cringe at such advice today because it is neither biblical nor practical. While strong attraction is not necessary to *keep* two people together, it is essential in *getting* two people together. Unless you feel you can't live without the other person, my best advice is to keep looking.

Why? As we saw in chapter 7, God uses our desires to provide guidance. "For it is God who is at work within you, giving you the will and the power to achieve his purpose" (Philippians 2:13, Phillips). We see the importance of desire in the story of Eliezer, Isaac, and Rebekah. Ultimately, Rebekah's marriage to Isaac didn't depend on Abraham's decree or Eliezer's decision but upon her desire: "And they [her family] said, 'We will call the girl and consult her wishes'" (Genesis 24:57).

Rebekah would have the final say about marrying Isaac. Although she never had seen him, she felt a strong, unmistakable desire to leave her family, travel more than five hundred miles to an unfamiliar country, and spend the rest of her life wedded to Isaac. While Eliezer depended on precepts, prayer, and practicality for guidance, Rebekah used her preference (desires) as an indicator of God's will.

While the absence of strong physical or emotional desires is no reason to end a marriage, it is a wonderful reason never to begin a marriage.

Principle #5: Trust in *Providence*

After all of Eliezer's efforts, what if Rebekah had said no? What if Abraham's servant had to return to Canaan empty-handed? Eliezer had actually voiced that concern to Abraham before he left on the journey: "Suppose the woman will not be willing to follow me to this land; should I take your son back to the land from where you came?" (Genesis 24:5).

Although Abraham fully believed that God would grant Eliezer success in his mission, he allowed for the possibility that God might have a different plan. "But if the woman is not willing to follow you, then you will be free from this my oath; only do not take my son back there" (Genesis 24:8).

Abraham was not expressing a lack of faith, but the essence of true faith. He was saying, "To the best of my ability I believe this is God's plan for securing Isaac's wife. But if for some reason it doesn't happen, I'm trusting that God will work it out another way." Faith isn't the hope that God will do what I want Him to do; it is the assurance that God will do what He wants to do in His way and in His time.

I love the title of a motivational book called *All You Can Do Is All You Can Do*. After we have obeyed God's precepts, engaged in prayer, exercised practicality, and consulted our preference, we must trust in God's providence in choosing a mate. If the other person says no, we can be confident that God has another plan. If the answer is yes, we can rest in the assurance that we've found God's perfect partner for us.

Work and the Will of God

Once you've found a mate, you'll need to determine how you'll survive as a couple. Caring and commitment are important for a successful marriage, but so is cash! Unless your Aunt Ethel has left you with a sizable trust fund, that means you and/or your mate will need to find a job. But how do you determine which career is God's will for your life?

The same principles we discussed in choosing a mate also apply in choosing a career. Let's assume that you're a Christian who is praying about this issue regularly. Let's also assume that you trust in God's sovereignty. You believe that ultimately His purpose will be accomplished. Beyond prayer and providence, let's explore three additional guides that are essential in discerning God's will about your vocation: principle, preference, and practicality.

1. Principle: "Every Job Is Important to God"

Somewhere along the way Christians have developed an unbiblical view of work. We either allow our work to become an idol that consumes our time and energy, or we view our work as a necessary evil (thanks to our forefather Adam) necessary to put bread on the table. Neither view is correct. In the opening pages of the Bible, we find God's view of work:

> And the Lord God planted a garden toward the east, in Eden; and there He placed the man whom He had formed.... Then the Lord God took the man and put him into the garden of Eden to cultivate it and keep it. (Genesis 2:8,15)

Remember, this was before Adam and Eve fell into sin, which caused our work to become much more difficult (see Genesis 3:17-19). God originally created a perfect garden, yet it was a garden that needed to be cultivated. Someone needed to mow the grass, plant the seeds, and harvest the produce. And Adam was designated to perform those tasks. It isn't that God really needed Adam. The Lord could have made the garden self-sustaining without any human intervention. Yet God fashioned the world in such a way that our own work is an extension of His original work of creation. Adam's work was a partnership with God.

It's significant that the first job God created had nothing to do with ministry. Adam wasn't called to be a preacher or a missionary, but instead a farmer and rancher. We're extremely short-sighted to limit "God's work" to church-related vocations. Yes, God does call men and women into specific ministries, but He also calls people to be farmers, teachers, lawyers, grocery store clerks, and truck drivers.

God's plan for the world certainly includes spreading the gospel of Jesus Christ, but His plan involves much more than that. For example, is God interested in providing food for His children? Does God care about the safety of His people? Does God desire that we have the necessary clothing? Then why is it so unusual to think that He would call some people to be farmers, others to be police officers, and others to be fashion designers?

Last week I traveled to Denver to lead a church's men's conference. My host for the weekend was a man who'd been a member of our church but had transferred to Denver with a major airline, where he supervises a number of other commercial pilots. While we were driving he said, "Robert, do you know what the most significant thing I ever remember you saying is?" I was sure he was going to mention some profound message on predestination or eschatology that I had delivered, but he had something else in mind. "I never will forget your saying that our jobs are important to God, not just as a platform from which to share the gospel, but as a way to serve Him."

My friend then took me to the top of a control tower at the Denver airport where we could see row after row of airplanes parked at their gates. Some were carrying mail, others were transporting medicine, others carried families to needed vacations or ministers to speaking engagements. Is God concerned about those details? Of course He is. But to accomplish His purpose, God needs truckers to transport the fuel, baggage handlers to load the cargo, pilots to fly the planes, and my friend to oversee the operation. I could understand why he saw his job as a calling from God.

Just as God gave Adam a specific assignment, God has given you a unique role to fill in His creation. Given the fact that we'll spend more than 60 percent of our waking hours at our jobs, it's important that we stop viewing work as a necessary evil. Instead, we need to understand work as our primary way of serving God. As A. W. Tozer wrote, "It is not what a man does that determines whether his work is sacred or secular, but why he does it."

2. Preference: "Do What You Want to Do"

Someone once said that "an unfulfilled vocation drains the color from a man's entire existence." I believe God wants us to do more than just endure life, He wants us to enjoy it. Our work is not only an assignment from God, it's also a gift that adds purpose and color to our existence. Solomon wrote:

> There is nothing better for a man than to eat and drink and tell himself that his labor is good. This also I have seen, that it is from the hand of God. For who can eat and who can have enjoyment without Him? (Ecclesiastes 2:24-25)

I find it significant that God did not say to Adam, "I want you to spend your entire day worshiping me. I want you to do nothing but sing hymns, pray, and meditate on My Word." God created Adam to be a worker as well as a worshiper. In the same way, the Lord has wired each of us in such a way that we need work to find fulfillment in life.

If God created us to be workers, then it should be no surprise that there is a correlation between our vocation and our desires. I believe that the primary method we should utilize in discovering our God-ordained assignment in life (whether it's a paying job or a volunteer position) is by examining our desires. Why? "[I]t is God who is at work within you, giving you the will and the power to achieve his purpose" (Philippians 2:13, Phillips).

In my book *Say Goodbye to Regret,* I wrote about discovering your "lifework," a term I learned from Bobb Biehl. He believes the single most important ingredient for experiencing satisfaction in your job is to discover your lifework—the vocation that is the best use of the rest of your life. How do you discover your lifework? Here are three questions you should ask yourself:

First, what needs in the world do I feel passionate about? Maybe as a child you were impressed by a particular teacher and since that time you've wanted to make a difference in other children's lives. Or possibly you're constantly daydreaming about starting a new business that will fulfill a unique niche in the marketplace. If God calls you to a particular vocation, He will give you "the will" to perform it.

Second, what's my single greatest strength? God not only gives us "the will" but also "the power" to do His work. God won't call you to be a doctor without giving you the necessary aptitude in science. He won't call you to be a public speaker without also giving you the ability to organize and communicate your thoughts.

Third, what do others say that I do best? When you've found your lifework, people will affirm you. They'll say, "You were born to do that" or "You make it look so easy." Conversely, when that affirmation is not present, you should reconsider your choice of vocation. Other people can provide valuable insight about our lifework. Remember, "Where there is no guidance, the people fall, [b]ut in abundance of counselors there is victory" (Proverbs 11:14).

3. Practicality: "Make Sure Your Job Pays the Bills"

I have a book on my shelf titled *Do What You Want and the Money Will Follow.* The author wisely advises readers to be more concerned about discovering their lifework than about making money. Those who discover their lifework usually discover that they also have an adequate income.

But the corollary is also true. God won't call you to a lifework that doesn't provide sufficient resources for you and your family. God wants your family to have adequate food, clothing, and shelter, and His primary way of providing for those needs is through your vocation. Consider Paul's words in 1 Timothy 5:8: "But if anyone does not provide for his own, and especially for those of his household, he has denied the faith, and is worse than an unbeliever."

Viewing your job as the channel through which God provides for your needs has two implications:

First, if you have a choice between employment and unemployment, choose employment. I've often counseled with people who say, "Since I'm no longer fulfilled in my job, I wonder if God is telling me to quit." "Do you have another job offer?" I inquire. "No, and furthermore I don't know how we'll pay our bills, but I know God doesn't want me to continue working at a job that makes me miserable." Wrong! While a job should invigorate us instead of debilitate us, eating still beats vocational fulfillment every time! That means you should stay at your job unless you have adequate reserves to sustain you for a lengthy period of time, or unless God has already provided another job.

Second, learn the difference between a hobby and a career. In one of my favorite *Seinfeld* episodes, the hapless George Costanza finds himself unemployed and seeks his friend's advice on a new career. "What do you like to do?" Jerry inquires. "Well, I like to go to the movies. And you know how I like to watch football games and make insightful comments,"

George answers. "That sounds interesting, but I'm not sure you can make a living doing that," Jerry advises.

A hobby is an activity that interests you; your lifework is an activity that provides you with an adequate income. For example, you may love fooling around with a computer and writing new programs, but can you pay the bills doing that? While money is not the only consideration in determining your lifework, it's one of the keys in choosing a vocation.

If you can utilize your talents and skills to do work you enjoy and it pays the bills, you've found your lifework. Several months ago I was talking with a young woman who was giving me a facial. (One of the occupational hazards of being on television is clogged pores from makeup.) Since I was in the middle of writing this chapter, I asked her what motivated her to choose her particular line of work.

"For years I worked in the corporate world and was absolutely miserable," she told me. "I dreaded pulling myself out of bed and going to work. Then I started asking myself what I really enjoyed doing most. I remembered that as a little girl I loved to work with people's skin. When I was ten, I would have my father lie down on the carpet and I would get all of my towels together and give him a facial. There was something about helping other people relax and at the same time knowing I was helping them that excited me. So I quit my job with the corporation, went back to beauty school, and now I'm having the time of my life." This young woman has discovered her lifework and is making a sufficient income to meet her needs. And by doing her work with enthusiasm and excellence, she is serving God. (After all, who wants to listen to a preacher with bad skin?)

By understanding the principle that all work is important to God, consulting the preferences that God has placed within your heart, and by exercising practicality in the choice of your vocation, you can discover with certainty your unique assignment in God's world. And once you discover that assignment, remember this: "Whatever you do, work at it with all your heart, as working for the Lord, not for men" (Colossians 3:23, NIV).

"Wait just a minute!" I hear some of you saying. "You're making it sound too easy. I've done everything you've suggested, and I still don't have any clear direction. Why doesn't God speak to me? And what am I supposed to do when He is silent?" If you've ever asked those questions, then the next chapter is for you.

9

God's Thundering Silence

What to do when the Lord refuses to speak

The telephone rang on Monday evening, interrupting another of our weekly family nights. Caller ID helps screen out the telemarketers, but when the caller is a parishioner, the technology can't identify the reason for the call.

That night the display read "hospital," so I knew the news probably wouldn't be good. The frantic voice on the other end of the line told me that one of the teenagers in our church had been killed in a freak traffic accident. I thanked the caller for the information and assured him I was on the way to the hospital.

Within a few minutes I arrived at the ER. The waiting area was filled with stunned family members and friends. A nurse and the hospital chaplain escorted me into a small room where the father, mother, and brother of the teenage girl stood around her lifeless body. For what seemed like an eternity, no one said a word. The only sounds were the muted yet powerful cries of anguish that can only come from a parent's heart. I thought of Rose Kennedy's observation that it's unnatural for parents to bury their children.

After a time of prayer together, the girl's mother asked a question for which she really expected no answer. "I know that God is in control. I'm not asking why He took our daughter. But I wish He would assure us that everything will be all right. Why doesn't God speak to us when we need Him the most?" Believe me, no pat answers would suffice. And I had none to offer anyway, since I've often asked the same questions.

Haven't you? If there really is a God in heaven who loves us and desires that the entire world know Him...

Why doesn't He reveal Himself through an audible voice or supernatural vision that everyone could experience?

Why doesn't He answer our prayers with a definite yes, no, or wait, instead of an ambiguous silence that is subject to misinterpretation?

Why doesn't He provide us with the clear, unmistakable guidance we request instead of allowing us to flounder in a fog of uncertainty?

I'm asking some of those questions this very week. Our church is considering whether to relocate to a different part of the city after 120 years at our current site. We're spending thousands of dollars hiring site-planning specialists, consultants, and architects to help us answer the question, "Should we stay where we are, or should we spend tens of millions of dollars to relocate?" One of the most spiritual men in our church asked me last week, "Robert, I know we need wise counsel from others, but shouldn't we spend our time seeking God's direction about this decision?"

To keep my pastoral image intact, I assured him that we certainly were praying about the matter. But I'm embarrassed to tell you what I really wanted to say: "God could spare us a lot of headaches if He'd simply tell us what to do. Instead, He's forcing us to waste all this time and money on consultants because He won't speak clearly to us."

Before you turn sanctimonious on me, I imagine you've experienced similar frustrations. There's no need to be embarrassed about it. Since the beginning of time some of the greatest men and women of faith have wrestled with God's thundering silence.

Think about Noah. From the time God told him to enter the ark until the time He allowed Noah to leave that massive boat, more than a year elapsed. Noah and his family endured 382 days of sheer terror as they heard the screams of people and animals being destroyed by the floodwaters, while they bobbed up and down in that floating barge. Yet during that time God didn't utter one word to Noah. This great man of faith must have wondered, "Where are you God? Have you forgotten us? Will I ever hear from You again?"

Or think about Abraham, the man God promised would be the father of a great nation. Yet more than a decade passed without any hint of a child or any reassuring word from God. So who could blame Abraham and Sara for taking matters into their own hands? Perhaps they'd heard one of those "God has no hands but our hands" sermons and decided to initiate their own plan. Sara encouraged her husband to have a one-night stand with her Egyptian servant, Hagar. The plan did produce a child, but the result was a disaster, both for Abraham's immediate family and the generations that would follow.

Abraham was eighty-six years old when Hagar bore his first son, Ishmael (Genesis 16:16). When he was ninety-nine, according to Genesis 17, the Lord appeared again to Abraham. That means God was silent for thirteen years after Abraham and Sara took matters into their own hands. I imagine during that period Abraham had some fairly hard questions for God:

"Why did You uproot me from my homeland and make a promise that You refuse to fulfill?"

"Why don't You answer my prayers and heal my fractured marriage?"

"Are You really capable of fulfilling Your promise? Do You even exist?"

No matter how fervently Abraham might have sought God's answers, his prayers were met with a thundering silence. Day after day, month after month, and year after year the heavens were quiet.

The great scholar F. B. Meyer offered an important insight about God's silence that is just as applicable today as it was more than a century ago when he penned these words:

> Some people are ever on the outlook for Divine appearances, for special manifestations, for celestial voices. Their life tends to be an incessant straining after some startling evidence of the nearness and the love of God. This feverishness is unwholesome and mistaken. Such manifestations are, indeed, delightful, but they are meant as bright surprises, and not as the rule of the Christian life: they are flung into our lives as a holiday into the school routine of a child. Yet, waiting on God to speak is to the heart what the long silence of winter is to the world of nature, in preparing for the outburst of spring.[1]

We don't like waiting for God to speak. We want some tangible evidence of His presence, and we want it *now*. I believe such a desire explains the explosive growth of Pentecostalism, which claims some 20 million adherents in the United States and 225 million around the world. People have a driving hunger and thirst to experience the presence of God.

There's nothing wrong with such a longing. David prayed, "O God, do not remain quiet; [d]o not be silent and, O God, do not be still" (Psalm 83:1). Yet in spite of their sincere desire to hear God, both David and Abraham experienced long periods of time in which God refused to speak.

During one particularly rough period in my life I memorized Psalm 34. The tone of the psalm strongly suggests that David was overflowing with gratitude to God for answering his prayers. David was obviously on a spiritual high when he penned these words:

> I will bless the LORD at all times;
> His praise shall continually be in my mouth.
> My soul shall make its boast in the LORD;
> The humble shall hear it and rejoice.

O magnify the Lord with me,
And let us exalt His name together.
I sought the Lord, and He answered me,
And delivered me from all my fears. (vv. 1-4)

Yet this same David also struggled through long periods during which God didn't even have the courtesy to say no to his requests for help. Instead, God answered David's prayers with a stubborn silence that provoked the psalmist to cry out:

My God, my God, why hast Thou forsaken me?
Far from my deliverance are the words of my groaning.
O my God, I cry by day, but Thou dost not answer;
And by night, but I have no rest. (Psalm 22:1-2)

You probably recognize these words as those spoken one thousand years later by Jesus Christ as He was suffocating on the cross. Have you ever considered the significance of the Son of God asking, "Where are You, God? Why don't You answer My prayers? Why have You turned Your back on Me?"

Jesus had obeyed God's laws perfectly. He had successfully resisted temptation. There was no sin in His life to confess. He had submitted Himself completely to His Father's will. And yet, in the last hour of His earthly life, He expressed profound dismay, distress, and disappointment with His Father.

I imagine you've been perplexed by God's silence when you desperately needed answers to help make sense of your pain. You can't understand why a heavenly Father who claims to be interested in your every action remains aloof when you desperately need His guidance. You need God's wisdom to know:

how to get out from under crushing debt;

what course of medical treatment to pursue for a life-threatening illness;

how to handle a boss's insistence that you overcharge a client for your services;

what to do about a spouse's suspected infidelity.

You've prayed about it. You've sought God's guidance. You're frantic for some answers. So why is God silent? If you sense some passion in these words, it's because I've struggled with God's slowness to answer my own prayers. When I advise people to pray about a particular issue, I keep my fingers crossed, hoping that God will "come through" and not damage His reputation. But as we've just seen, God's past dealings with His people indicate that He's not a heavenly bellhop who feels obligated to answer the moment we ring the bell. Instead, the divine pattern seems to suggest that silence is the rule rather than the exception.

Still, the Scriptures promise guidance from God when we ask:

> Trust in the LORD with all your heart,
> And do not lean on your own understanding.
> In all your ways acknowledge Him,
> And He will make your paths straight. (Proverbs 3:5-6)

> But if any of you lacks wisdom, let him ask of God, who gives to all men generously and without reproach, and it will be given to him. (James 1:5)

How do we reconcile God's promises for guidance with His thundering silence? Some would resolve the conflict by pointing out (as I did in chapter 3) that God is never really silent. He not only has spoken through His Word, He still is speaking through His Word. The writer of Hebrews tells us that the Word of God is living, not dead; it is active, not passive. That means:

When I tell God I'm lonely, He answers (Hebrews 13:5);

When I tell God I'm worried, He invites me to cast all my cares on Him (1 Peter 5:7);

When I tell God I'm concerned about taking care of my family's financial needs, He promises to supply all of my needs (Philippians 4:19);

When I tell God I'm afraid of dying, He assures me that He will take me to be with Him (John 14:3).

Let's be honest. As wonderful as the promises of the Bible are, there are times that they just don't seem to apply to the dilemma we're facing. President Ronald Reagan's biographer recounts an incident during the president's latter years in office when his powers of concentration were diminishing. At a crucial summit meeting, the prime minister of Iceland asked Reagan if he'd consider prohibiting the shipment of dangerous chemicals that threatened Iceland's environment. Unprepared for such a question, the president reached into his coat pocket and retrieved some prepared index cards. Then he began to read, "I'm very happy to be able to tell you, Mr. Prime Minister, that Icelandair [the national airline of Iceland] will be granted landing rights in Boston." While the prime minister appreciated the president's statement, it had nothing to do with his pressing question.[2]

Reasons for God's Silence

Maybe you've immersed yourself in the Scriptures seeking the answer to an urgent question, then felt like the only direction you received had nothing to do with your pressing need. The Bible is full of wonderful promises and general guidance, so why does God remain silent when we ask for help? The Bible provides at least four explanations.

Unconfessed Sin

The downside of writing books is that once printed, your words can't be retrieved. I've written some words in the past that I wish I could delete or at least amend. For example, in an earlier work I dealt with seven common myths about prayer that hindered people from praying. One of those myths was that "God will not answer my prayers if there is any unconfessed sin in my life." I reasoned that if all of a Christian's sins—past, present, and future—have been totally forgiven, those sins could no longer inhibit our communication with God. I still believe we shouldn't wait until we feel our lives are perfect before we talk with God. Prayer is often the road that leads us back into a right relationship with our heavenly Father.

However, I should have made a clearer distinction between God's judicial forgiveness and His parental forgiveness. When we become Christians, God grants us judicial forgiveness. In the great courtroom of heaven we are declared not guilty on the basis of Christ's death for us. But such forgiveness doesn't exempt us from experiencing God's parental disapproval for our sins.

When one of my girls disobeys me, I don't disown her or turn her out onto the street to fend for herself. She's my daughter and nothing will ever change that fact. Nevertheless, until my daughter is willing to admit that she's wrong, there will be a breach in our relationship. I have little interest in answering her request for spending money or providing help in solving a dilemma she's facing at school. Why? Although my daughter wants to ignore her disobedience and pretend that all is well between us, I want her to understand that there's a problem that must be resolved before we can resume a normal relationship.

In the same way, the Bible teaches that our sin disrupts God's communication with us.

> But your iniquities have made a separation between you and your
> God,
> And your sins have hidden His face from you, so that He does not
> hear. (Isaiah 59:2)

> For the eyes of the Lord are upon the righteous,
> And His ears attend to their prayer,
> But the face of the Lord is against those who do evil. (1 Peter 3:12)

What husband or wife has not used silence to awaken an otherwise oblivious mate to an unresolved offense? Eventually the lack of responsiveness will elicit the desired "What's wrong, dear?" and the offended party will be more than happy to answer! In the same way, God sometimes refuses to answer our requests in order to alert us to a problem in our relationship with Him.

But at other times sin prevents our hearing God's voice, so He appears silent when in fact He is still speaking. Many years ago I served as an associate minister at a large metropolitan church, but I knew that eventually I would become a senior pastor. During that time, a congregation in West Texas asked me if I would consider becoming their pastor. After meeting with the search committee, my wife, Amy, and I got into our car to head home. Before I started the engine, she asked, "Robert, what do you think?" I replied, "I have zero interest in going to that church." With tears streaming down her face, she replied, "I believe God is leading us there."

She couldn't understand why I didn't sense God's Spirit in the meeting, and I couldn't fathom why she felt so strongly about leaving a huge church in a thriving metropolis to go to a small church for an even smaller salary. If I was going to sacrifice a comfortable situation, I wanted to go to a "substantial" church, not one my friends and associates had never heard of. In the months that followed, it was evident that God was leading us to that wonderful congregation where we experienced God's supernatural blessing for seven years.

Why didn't I initially sense God's leading in the same way my wife had? God obviously was speaking to both of us, but I allowed my own selfish ambitions to affect my ability to hear God's voice. I was a poster boy for the double-minded man described in James 1:6-8. I sincerely wanted God's direction in my life, but I also had an insatiable thirst for success that prevented me from hearing Him, even though He was speaking clearly.

What sin are you clinging to that is preventing you from hearing God's voice? Unbridled ambition? An exhilarating but immoral relationship? Unresolved bitterness toward someone who has wronged you? An unhealthy habit that is slowly destroying your life? Greed that has become the focus of your life?

Ask God to reveal the specific sin in your life that is drowning out His clear voice. But then, I bet you already know the answer.

Uncontrolled Emotions

If you have girls living in your home, then you know that the caring and tending of hair is a major pastime: washing it, styling it, and occasionally cursing it. Part of the nightly ritual around our place is allowing our girls to dry their hair while my wife and I enjoy a television program. But as soon as the whir of the dryer begins, I reach for the remote control and crank up the volume. Why? Not because there is no sound coming from the television. I can clearly hear every word—until the shrill sound of the hair dryer begins.

In the same way, certain emotions that erupt inside of us can drown out God's voice. Morton Kelsey has written:

> Out of silence, disturbing emotions often come to the surface which are difficult to control. They can range from vague apprehension to

> terror and panic, or they may vary from bitterness and indignation to aggressive hatred and rage. Usually we attach these feelings to some object in the outer world, something we do not really need to fear, or someone who deserves our compassion rather than our anger. Most of our lives are constricted by half-conscious fears of some kind that keep us from dealing adequately with the world around us.[3]

Of all the emotions that compete with God's voice, none is more powerful than fear. Maybe you've sensed that God is leading you to move to a different city, to change vocations, to marry a specific person, or to enter full-time ministry. But the two most paralyzing words in the English language have overtaken your emotions: what if. What if I move my family to that city and my children are unhappy? What if I take this new job and the company goes bankrupt? What if I marry this person and it doesn't work out? What if I enter the ministry but no church ever calls me?

If you've experienced such doubts, it might encourage you to know that some of the greatest men and women in the Bible also battled fear. For example, Abraham is a guy whose picture appears in the dictionary next to the word *faith.* And yet Abraham's faith was sometimes extinguished by anxiety.

In Genesis 14 we read of Abraham's daring rescue of his nephew Lot from the kings of the east. The king of Sodom was so grateful for Abraham's intervention that he offered the patriarch great riches. But Abraham refused that wealth so no one would doubt that God was his benefactor.

But then Abraham starting playing the "what if" game. What if the kings of the east regroup and attack me and my family? What if my wife leaves me for a wealthier man? What if the money in my IRA isn't sufficient to take care of my retirement needs?

Suddenly Abraham was doubting what had appeared to be God's clear leading in his life. So the Lord told him, "Do not fear, Abram, I am a shield to you; [y]our reward shall be very great" (Genesis 15:1).

God was saying to His closest friend on earth, "Don't worry. I've built a hedge around you. Nothing will happen to you without My permission. Not only that, but I'll reward you in My way and in My time."

God says the same thing to you and to me. When Satan bombards us with a barrage of "what ifs" that cause us to question God's direction in our lives, the only answer is to hold up that shield of faith that says, "God is my protector. He won't allow anything in my life that doesn't bear His stamp of approval."

Unpredictable Timing

Sometimes God's silence is only a perceived silence due to our unconfessed sin or our uncontrolled emotions. But at other times God appears to be silent because He *is* silent. He chooses not to answer our request for guidance or intervention because He is not yet ready to act.

Remember the story of Lazarus, the brother of Mary and Martha? Lazarus became desperately ill, so his sisters sent word to Jesus about their brother's condition. Being women of faith, they had no doubt that if Jesus knew of Lazarus's illness, He would immediately come and heal His close friend. But John records a different response from Jesus. "Now Jesus loved Martha, and her sister, and Lazarus. When therefore He heard that he was sick, He stayed then two days longer in the place where He was" (John 11:5-6).

You can almost hear Martha's inner struggles: "Wait a minute! If Jesus loves us so much, why'd He refuse our request for healing? Why would He allow our brother to die? With friends like *that*, who needs…?" When the Lord finally arrived, Martha ran to Him, saying, "What took You so long? If You'd been here earlier, my brother wouldn't have died!"

Martha failed to comprehend that Jesus had a purpose and timetable that were different from hers. Her goal was immediate healing; Jesus' goal was ultimate healing, not only for Lazarus but for all who would believe in Him. Part of His plan for fulfilling that purpose was allowing Lazarus to die so that Jesus might raise him from the dead, affirming His deity. There were two distinct goals that resulted in two different timetables.

Or think about Moses. Early in life he sensed that God was calling him to deliver His people from Egypt after they had suffered hundreds of years of slavery. Yet the years passed and nothing happened. So Moses unwisely took matters into his own hands.

> But when he was approaching the age of forty, it entered his mind to visit his brethren, the sons of Israel. And when he saw one of them being treated unjustly, he defended him and took vengeance for the oppressed by striking down the Egyptian. And he supposed that his brethren understood that God was granting them deliverance through him; but they did not understand. (Acts 7:23-25)

You know the rest of the story. Because of his impatience with God's timing, Moses spent the next forty years on the backside of the desert tending sheep. No doubt Moses thought God was through with him.

Try placing yourself in his sandals. Forty years in a strange land with no word from God. Moses certainly must have thought God had benched him forever. His days of ministry were obviously over. But the Bible says, "Now it came about in the course of those many days that the king of Egypt died. And the sons of Israel sighed because of the bondage.... So God heard their groaning" (Exodus 2:23-24).

One day without warning, while Moses was tending to his chores, God appeared to him in a burning bush and said, "It's time." That's how God works. He speaks only when He is ready. The silence you're experiencing from heaven may have nothing to do with sin in your life or uncontrolled emotions or even lack of faith. Instead, God is not yet ready to answer your request. But one day, a day that will begin like every other day, God will suddenly speak loudly and clearly.

Undeveloped Faith

If God loves us and wants what is best for us, why doesn't He quickly answer our requests for guidance? Ben Patterson may have the answer. He believes the things God does for us while we wait are as important as the thing we're waiting for. Waiting is not just something we endure until God acts on our behalf; waiting is part of the process of our becoming what God wants us to be.[4] Sören Kierkegaard said that Christians are like school children who want to look up the answers to their math problems in the back of the book instead of working through those problems.[5] But contrary to our desires, the real learning occurs in the struggle.

The one quality that God is most interested in developing in us is faith. "And without faith it is impossible to please Him," the Bible tells us (Hebrews 11:6). What is faith? It's the assurance that God is going to do what He has promised to do. And the only way He can develop that faith in us is through the struggle of waiting. As the apostle Paul wrote, "And not only this, but we also exult in our tribulations, knowing that tribulation brings about perseverance; and perseverance, proven character; and proven character, hope" (Romans 5:3-4).

In his book *Sabbatical Journeys,* the late Henri Nouwen wrote about some friends who were trapeze artists. The Flying Roudellas explained to Henri that there must exist a very special relationship between the flier and the catcher in the trapeze act. Obviously, the flier (the one who lets go) is totally dependent on the catcher (the one who grabs hold of the flier). In the act, there comes that critical moment when the flier releases the bar. He arcs out into the air, and his responsibility is to remain absolutely still, to wait for the hands of the catcher. The trapeze artist told Nouwen, "The flier must never try to catch the catcher." Instead, he must wait in stillness for the catcher to do his work.[6]

In the same way God says to us, "Rest in the Me and wait patiently for Me. Be still and know that I am God. I will not allow you to stumble or fall."

V. Raymond Edman, the late president of Wheaton College, described a period in his life when God seemed distant and silent:

> Something painful happened to me. This is how I met it: I was quiet for a while with the Lord, and then I wrote these words for myself:
>
> First, He brought me here. It is by His will I am in this strait place: in that fact I will rest.
>
> Next, He will keep me here in His love, and give me grace as His child.
>
> Then, He will make the trial a blessing, teaching me the lessons He intends me to learn, and working in me the grace He needs to bestow.
>
> Last, in His good time He can bring me out again—how and when only He knows.
>
> Let me say I am here, first, by God's appointment; second, in His keeping; third, under His training; fourth, for His time.[7]

You might be experiencing the thundering silence of God at this very moment. Regardless of how you feel about Him, He hasn't changed His feeling about you, and neither has He forgotten you. Remember, you are where you are by His appointment; you are in His keeping; you are undergoing His training; and, He *will* eventually speak...in His way and in His time.

10

The Shepherd's Safety Net

What you can know when you make the wrong *decision*

Remember Bill and Sally Newcomb? They were the couple we met in chapter 1 who were considering a job opportunity in another city. Out of the blue they received an offer from an old friend to join him in a new Internet toy business. The recent restlessness they had experienced, coupled with the potential financial rewards of this new venture, made them wonder if perhaps God was orchestrating this move.

However, their pastor's sermon about discovering God's will left them with more questions than answers. They could see how the Bible, prayer, circumstances, counsel, and personal desires could make an argument for either staying *or* leaving. Either choice would be equally honoring to God. So what were they to do?

Several weeks after hearing the sermon on God's will, the Newcombs heard another message from their pastor entitled "Moving Out of Your Comfort Zone." Using God's call to Abraham to leave his home country for a new land that God would show him, the pastor made the following application: "Some of you have grown too comfortable in your present situation. There are few surprises in your life. Before the morning dawns, you can predict the majority of your day ranging from the events at work to the conversation around the dinner table. With that predictability comes a lack of dependence on God. Why do you need to trust Him when your life is so under control?

"But God is getting ready to move some of you out of your comfort zone. You're beginning to sense that He is leading you away from the familiar present to an uncertain future. And the only guarantee He offers you are two simple words: 'Trust Me.' "

Outside of skywriting, how could God speak any more clearly? That afternoon, Bill called Jerry and accepted the job offer. Sensing God's definite direction, the Newcomb family headed out of state for their long-awaited promised land.

But within a year Sally and Bill realized they had traded their comfort zone for the Twilight Zone. Their oldest son, Matt, who'd been an honor student throughout his eleven years in school, was struggling to maintain a passing average. Sally strongly suspected that her freshman daughter, Mandy, was sexually involved with a boy she'd met at her new school. Bill and Sally had been unable to sell their old house, condemning them to months of double mortgage payments and strangling their cash flow.

If all of those circumstances weren't enough, Bill's new business was on the brink of bankruptcy. Two weeks after the Newcombs moved, the major investor who'd promised to provide the majority of the start-up capital got cold feet. As a result, the fledgling company was facing financial failure.

Normally, Bill and Sally would have found support from their church. But the church they attended in their new city had just suffered a major split, and the few friends they'd made were more interested in offering condemnation for the other side than in providing comfort for newcomers. Bill and Sally were disillusioned with life in general and with God in particular. They had some serious questions that no one seemed willing or able to answer: "How could we have so misread God's leading? Why would God allow us to make such a terrible mistake? Is God some kind of heavenly sadist who's playing a cruel trick on us?"

Perhaps you picked up this book because you're facing a tough decision of your own. You might be considering a proposal of marriage, a relocation, or a call to the ministry. Like the Newcombs, you've considered the principles we've discussed in this book. God's Word, prayer, counsel, circumstances, and your own desires are causing you to lean toward a specific course of action. Like the flier in the trapeze act we discussed in the last chapter, you're about to let go of the security of your present situation and arc out into the air. But before you do, you wonder, "How can I keep from making a serious mistake? How can I know for sure that what I'm hearing is really the Master's voice?"

Amid the uncertainty of difficult choices is one unchanging truth that we can rely on. God's sovereignty is stretched out underneath our every decision and circumstance, and even our mistakes. That is the eternal, unchanging safety net that God provides.

Understanding God's Plan

Every time I speak to our congregation about the sovereignty of God (especially when the message contains words such as *election* and *predestination*), I get a little gun-shy. I can't help but recall an earlier experience in my ministry. I hadn't been pastor at my first church very long when a small group decided to get rid of me. One Sunday I was preaching from Romans 9: "So then it does not depend on the man who wills or the man who runs, but on God who has mercy.... So then He has mercy on whom He desires, and He hardens whom He desires" (vv. 16,18).

After my message, the dissenters felt they had the smoking gun necessary to convict and sentence me. At a deacon's meeting called the following Tuesday, they ambushed me with a host of accusations. "Your kind of preaching discourages evangelism. Your message denies the free choice that God gives every person. If what you're saying is true, then we're nothing but robots."

Perhaps you've heard (or even voiced) similar objections to teachings on God's sovereignty. While a detailed explanation of this doctrine falls outside the parameters of this book, we need to examine the relationship between God's sovereignty and His purpose for our lives.

What do we mean when we say God is sovereign? In general, the sovereignty of God refers to His rule over creation. God alone is in control. His claim that "I am the Lord, and there is no other" (Isaiah 45:6) guarantees that His all-inclusive plan for His creation will be fulfilled. Nothing can thwart what God wants to accomplish. Adam and Eve's sin in the garden, the rebellion of the Israelites in the wilderness, the Holocaust, and the tornado that ravages a community all fall under the reign of God. Nothing takes Him by surprise. And more important, nothing can force Him to alter His plan.

A few years ago I heard about a giant asteroid that came "dangerously close" (within a half million miles) to our planet. Experts claim that a collision with this asteroid would have equaled the impact of fifty thousand hydrogen bombs. Yet God, who upholds all things by the power of His Word, kept it from striking the earth. The same God who keeps the paths of planets and asteroids in check will also prevent any "accidents" in your life. In terms of the decisions you face, God's sovereignty means that He will accomplish His plan for your life.

"What if I choose the wrong mate?" God will accomplish His plan for your life.

"What if I mistake a random circumstance as God's direction?" God will accomplish His plan for your life.

"What if I rebel against God?" He will accomplish His plan for your life.

God has a purpose for your life that won't be compromised by your circumstances, your mistakes, or even your rebellion. Hard to believe? Actually, that truth is not as preposterous as it seems when you consider two truths about God: He has a plan, and He has the power to accomplish His plan.

God has a plan. One of my staff members is the epitome of organization. Every appointment is carefully entered into his electronic daytimer, his schedule is organized by fifteen-minute intervals, and his presentations to our lay leaders are accompanied by voluminous handouts covering the most minute details. It's interesting to watch the differing reactions to his penchant for planning. Those who are highly organized love his efforts. But others who are less disciplined have difficulty understanding him. "He needs to relax and not take things so seriously," they counsel. Similarly, some people have difficulty believing that God would plot every detail in His creation simply because they don't appreciate the importance of planning.

But should it surprise us that a perfect God would have an intricate design for His vast creation? My former pastor, W. A. Criswell, once observed,

> Before a stone was laid in the construction of St. Paul's Cathedral in London, the idea was born in the mind of Sir Christopher Wren. He saw it in his mind and purposed it in his heart. Before he struck a chisel against the heavy rock of marble, Michaelangelo saw the mighty Moses in his mind and purposed it in his heart. Before there was a stroke of the brush against the canvas, the young artist Raphael saw the spectacular picture of the Sistine Madonna in his mind. Why should it surprise us then that God, the designer and architect of the universe, should have a plan and purpose for His creation? The greater the project, the more necessary the plan.[1]

The apostle Paul described the detailed plan of God when he wrote, "[A]lso we have obtained an inheritance, having been predestined according to His purpose who works *all things* after the counsel of His will" (Ephesians 1:11).

Paul says all things fall under God's sovereign plan. That plan includes the decrees of the president (Proverbs 21:1), the outcome of the rolled dice (Proverbs 16:33), and the change of seasons (Daniel 2:21). But as we have seen in previous chapters, God's plan also includes the smallest details of *your* life. The color of your eyes, the number of hairs on your head, and even the bent of your emotions all are part of God's design. The psalmist recognized this truth when he wrote:

> For Thou didst form my inward parts;
> Thou didst weave me in my mother's womb.
> I will give thanks to Thee, for I am fearfully and wonderfully made;
> Wonderful are Thy works,
> And my soul knows it very well. (Psalm 139:13-14)

God's plan not only involves those areas of life beyond our control (our race, our birthplace, our genetic makeup), but also those parts of our life we think are under our control. For example, we assume that we determine the use of our time. Whether we watch television, read the paper, mow the grass, play tennis, or go to the grocery store is a matter of our discretion—or so we think. But listen to what the writer of Proverbs claims:

> Man's steps are ordained by the LORD,
> How then can man understand his way? (Proverbs 20:24)

Every step you take and every move you make is part of God's detailed blueprint for your life. And yes—as the writer says—such a thought is beyond our comprehension. But it is a truth that offers us tremendous security.

Last week I left work early to get a haircut. As I drove to the barbershop, I passed through an intersection and within seconds I heard the screeching of brakes. I glanced in my rearview mirror and saw the car behind me decimated by another vehicle running a red light. I pulled to the side of the road and dialed 911 for assistance, but it was too late. The driver was dead.

Believe me, I spent a while processing what I'd just seen. What if I'd left work two seconds later? What if it had taken me just a little longer to get to that intersection? What if the driver who ran the red light had been traveling a little faster? My life would have been snuffed out instantly. Suddenly I was more aware—and grateful—that I had less control over my steps than I had assumed. God has a plan for my life that includes not only the day of my birth, but also the day of my death.

> And in Thy book they were all written,
> The days that were ordained for me,
> When as yet there was not one of them. (Psalm 139:16)

Obviously, that one facet of God's plan requires many other smaller plans to ensure that I don't leave this planet one second before my appointed time. Don't you find it comforting to know that Someone wiser and more powerful than you is guiding every detail of your life?

Jeremiah was one of God's most faithful prophets during the twilight years of the kingdom of Judah. He endured violent opposition, beatings, and imprisonment without wavering in his prophetic assignment. What was the source of his courage? He was grounded in the knowledge that God wouldn't allow any accidents in his life. Read the words of assurance that God offered Jeremiah at the beginning of his ministry:

> Before I formed you in the womb I knew you,
> And before you were born I consecrated you;
> I have appointed you a prophet to the nations. (Jeremiah 1:5)

Eugene Peterson skillfully expresses the profound implications of this verse with these words:

> Before Jeremiah knew God, God knew Jeremiah: "Before I formed you in the womb I knew you." This turns everything we ever thought about God around....
>
> We enter a world we didn't create. We grow into a life already provided for us.... If we are going to live appropriately, we must be aware that we are living in the middle of a story that was begun and will be concluded by another. And this other is God....
>
> Jeremiah's life didn't start with Jeremiah. Jeremiah's salvation didn't start with Jeremiah. Jeremiah's truth didn't start with Jeremiah. He entered the world in which the essential parts of his existence were already ancient history. So do we. "I knew you."[2]

We've established that God has a detailed plan for each of our lives. But that's just the beginning. A second truth is crucial to understanding God's sovereignty as it relates to His will for each of us.

God has the power to accomplish His plan. Some people would concede that a perfect God would have a plan encompassing every detail of His creation. "But," they would add, "sometimes man or Satan ruins God's perfect plan. That's why God has two wills: His *perfect* will and His *permissive* will." When you ask for examples of the permissive will of God, people generally list everything for which they have no easy answers: starving babies, devastating floods, and undeserved suffering. Since we can't understand how a good and loving God could have any involvement with such tragedies, we attempt to let God off the hook with dichotomies between His perfect and permissive will.

But such a distinction isn't found in the Bible. God doesn't have to settle for second best. He isn't semisovereign. He alone is sovereign over His creation. He has the power to fulfill His ultimate plan.

Remember how the Old Testament patriarch Job suffered the loss of his children, his possessions, and his health? He understandably had some serious questions about God's role in his tragic circumstances. But read his conclusion regarding God's absolute sovereignty: "I know that Thou canst do all things, [a]nd that no purpose of Thine can be thwarted" (Job 42:2). Job was saying, "God, I don't pretend to understand what You are up to in my life. But I believe that You have a plan, even though I can't see what that plan is."

Our Responsibilities

Before we look at the implications of God's sovereignty in our decision making, it's important to clarify what God's sovereignty does *not* imply. While God has a perfect plan, and while He has the power to accomplish His plan, that doesn't give us the freedom to coast. We still are responsible for and held accountable for certain things.

1. We still must make wise choices. A young man came to the late Bible teacher J. Vernon McGee and said, "Dr. McGee, I've been studying predestination, and I'm so convinced of the sovereignty of God that I believe that if I stood in the middle of a busy highway, and my hour had not yet come, God would spare my life." McGee replied in his trademark manner, "Son, if you stand in the middle of a busy highway, your hour *has* come."

The safety net of God's sovereignty doesn't exclude us from the responsibility of searching the Scriptures for God's principles, seeking God in prayer, and soliciting the best counsel we can receive before we make a decision.

2. We still suffer the natural consequences of our actions and decisions. A failure to obey God's precepts and principles results in very real and painful results. For example, consider the death of Jesus. On Friday afternoon as the apostles watched their dreams of the last three years evaporate, I'm sure they were tempted to think "What a tragedy! Why didn't God intervene and stop Pilate from crucifying the Messiah? Jesus' death may have been a part of God's permissive will, but it certainly couldn't have been God's *perfect* will."

Yet the passing of a few weeks (not to mention an empty tomb) changed the apostles' perspective on God's will. Within several months of Christ's death, the apostles preached: "For truly in this city there were gathered together against Thy holy servant Jesus, whom Thou didst anoint, both Herod and Pontius Pilate, along with the Gentiles and the peoples of Israel, to do whatever Thy hand and Thy purpose predestined to occur" (Acts 4:27-28).

Jesus' death was no accident. The crucifixion was not Plan B in God's eternal plan. Calvary was God's perfect will that was accomplished through imperfect men. Although God had predetermined when, how, and by whom Christ would be put to death, Herod and Pilate still had to suffer the eternal consequences for making a very bad choice.

3. We still face difficult questions that have no clear answers. How could Pilate be held responsible for Christ's death if God had predestined it? How can God hold unbelievers accountable for their rejection of Christ if He predestines those who will be saved? How can God fulfill His plan for my life in spite of my mistakes and even my rebellion against Him?

The honest answer is, "I don't know—and neither does anyone else." Beware of any theological system that attempts to reconcile the two irreconcilable truths (in this life) of God's sovereignty and man's responsibility. One person has wisely observed: "Try to explain predestination, and you will lose your mind. Try to explain it away, and you may lose your soul."

The Benefits of God's Sovereignty

While it's impossible for our finite minds to comprehend the workings of an infinite God, we can identify some tangible benefits that come from trusting in God's sovereignty—especially when we're seeking to know God's will for our lives.

1. God's sovereignty offers me peace from the past. Yesterday I counseled with a husband whose marriage had dissolved after more than twenty years. "If only I had been the kind of spiritual leader I needed to be," he lamented, "I would still have my wife and my children." I assured him that in spite of the wrong choices he'd made, God still was in control. When God promises to work "all things together for good," the "all things" includes our mistakes and even our outright rebellion against Him. Such a truth frees us from the paralyzing "if onlys" of our wrong decisions.

In commenting on the life of David, who made his share of wrong choices, Chuck Swindoll observes, "When a man or woman of God fails, nothing of God fails. When a man or woman of God changes, nothing of God changes. When someone dies, nothing of God dies. When our lives are altered by the unexpected, nothing of God is altered or unexpected."[3]

2. God's sovereignty offers comfort for the present. Matthew 14 recounts the familiar story of Jesus' stilling the storm that threatened His disciples' safety. In the middle of the storm, Jesus suddenly appeared to His disciples. Wondering whether it was really the Lord, Peter cried out, "Lord, if it is You, command me to come to You on the water" (v. 28).

You know the rest of the story. Peter ventured out of the boat and stayed afloat for about two seconds until he started looking at the boiling sea around him. When he began to sink, he uttered the shortest plea recorded in the Bible: "Lord, save me!" (v. 30). Not a prayer heavy on theology, yet filled with practicality!

But notice *how* Jesus saved Peter: "[I]mmediately Jesus stretched out

His hand and took hold of him, and said to him, 'O you of little faith, why did you doubt?' And when they got into the boat, the wind stopped" (vv. 31-32).

The order of events is crucial. Jesus didn't first still the storm and then save Peter. Instead, the Lord grabbed Peter's hand and walked with him through the storm as it continued to rage around them. Only after Jesus safely delivered Peter into the boat did He quiet the storm.

Maybe you're experiencing a similar situation. Things were progressing well until suddenly, out of nowhere, dark clouds appeared, the lightning began to flash, the thunderclouds clapped, and you found yourself in the middle of a fierce storm. As the winds of adversity howl around you and the unrelenting rains of discouragement pour down, your visibility is limited. "Where is God in all of this? If He really exists, why doesn't He deliver me out of this storm?"

So often we ask God to still the storm, to change our circumstances. Certainly a sovereign God is capable of doing just that. His hand is strong enough to heal the body that has fallen ill or to change the heart that has grown cold. Yet my experience is that God rarely changes our situation. Instead of delivering us *out of* the storm, He walks with us *through* the storm. And when His sovereign plan is accomplished, He causes the winds to subside as quickly as they began.

3. God's sovereignty offers us assurance for the future. The prophet Daniel promised, "[T]he people who know their God will display strength and take action" (Daniel 11:32). Once I've followed the principles of guidance we've discussed in this book, the truth of God's sovereignty gives me the boldness to act, knowing that my decision—right or wrong—won't alter God's good and perfect plan for my life. What confidence, what freedom such a truth provides!

A. W. Tozer described that freedom when he wrote:

> To the child of God, there is no such thing as accident. He travels an appointed way. The path he treads was chosen for him when as yet he was not, when as yet he had existence only in the mind of God. Accidents may indeed appear to befall him and misfortune stalks his way; but these evils will be so in appearance only and will seem evils only because we cannot read the secret script of God's hidden providence and so cannot discover the ends at which He aims.
>
> The [person] of true faith may live in the absolute assurance that his steps are ordered by the Lord. For him, misfortune is outside the bounds of possibility. He cannot be torn from this earth one hour ahead of the time God has appointed, and he cannot be detained on earth one moment after God is done with him here. He is not a waif on the wide world, a foundling of time and space, but a saint of the Lord and the darling of His particular care.[4]

Some time after Tozer penned those words, a Methodist reader wrote to the great preacher questioning his theology about predestination and relegating such beliefs to the Presbyterian church. Tozer responded:

> Dear Brother: When I said we traveled an appointed way I was not thinking about foreordination, predestination, eternal security, or eternal decrees. I was just thinking about how nice it is for the steps of a good man to be ordered by the Lord; and that if a consecrated Christian will put himself in the hands of God, even the accidents will be turned into blessings.... I am sure the Methodist brother can go to sleep tonight knowing that he does not have to turn Presbyterian to be certain that God is looking after him.[5]

And isn't that the bottom line for every one of us? We have a Great Shepherd who loves us, who guides us, and who cares for us. And even when we stray from Him, our movement is limited by the boundaries of His love and His perfect will. Jesus promised us: "My sheep hear My voice, and I know them, and they follow Me; and I give eternal life to them, and they shall never perish; and no one shall snatch them out of My hand" (John 10:27-28).

What a promise for those who seek to follow the Master's voice!

For Further Reflection

Study Questions on God's Will

Chapter 1: Where There's God's Will, There Must Be a Way

1. What advice would you give to Bill and Sally Newcomb, the couple considering a move to another city?
2. Do you agree with the book Rachel Jenkins read that claims God has no particular blueprint for every decision in our lives? Why or why not?
3. Have you had an experience like Darla Everett's in which you thought you'd heard God speak, but later you discovered you were mistaken? What did you learn from that experience?
4. Why do you think the subject of discovering God's will is of such interest to so many people?
5. Which, if any, of the three most common approaches to discovering God's will (formulaic, rational, experiential) do you tend to use? Why? Have you been successful in discerning God's will for your life?
6. What is the most pressing decision you are facing right now? Do you believe God has a specific desire concerning that decision? How can you discover God's will in this area?
7. What prompted you to start reading this book? What do you hope to gain from this study?

Chapter 2: Scrutinizing the Inscrutable

1. Do you agree with George Mueller's statement at the beginning of the chapter? Have you ever sincerely asked God for direction and failed to receive it?
2. Explain the three different uses of the term "God's will"—providential, preceptive, and personal.
3. Do you believe that God has a sovereign will for your life that can't be changed? Why or why not?
4. Think about a major decision you're facing. Can you give specific examples of how God's preceptive will applies to your decision?
5. Do you believe in a personal will of God that affects every area of your life, or do you tend to agree with those who say that no such specific blueprint exists? Why or why not?
6. Which of the author's arguments are strongest for supporting the idea of a personal will of God? Which are the weakest?
7. Of the variety of methods God has used in the past to communicate His will to His people, which do you think are most effective for hearing His voice today? Do you believe God uses all of those methods today? Why or why not?
8. The author says that God rarely reveals every step we need to take, but He will always reveal the next step we need to take. What is the most pressing dilemma you're facing right now? How do you expect God to reveal the next step to you?

Chapter 3: The Bible Tells Me So?

1. Why do you think Christians often ignore the Bible when they're searching for direction?
2. Cite an example from you own experience in which the Bible was

helpful in providing direction. Have there been other times when the Bible provided *little* help to you in determining God's will? Why?

3. What do you believe is the most convincing evidence that the Bible can be trusted as God's perfect Word?
4. Imagine that a friend said to you, "God appeared to me in a dream and told me that I should divorce my mate." Assuming that there are no clear biblical reasons for this divorce, what would you say to your friend? Does personal revelation that seems to be from God ever supersede biblical mandates? Why or why not?
5. The author mentions three ways people misuse the Bible. Have you ever attempted to use the Bible in one of these ways (to predict the future, to answer all of your questions, or to provide specific answers)? What was the result of such misuse?
6. How would you answer a new Christian who asked, "Why do we only follow some of the laws in the Old Testament and not all of them?"
7. Do you have a plan for reading God's Word? Has your plan changed through the years? As you look back, what plan has yielded the greatest results?
8. What is the single greatest barrier you are facing in developing a regular program for reading and meditating on God's Word? Identify one or two specific steps you can take today to remove that barrier.

CHAPTER 4: OUR AMAZING LISTENING GOD

1. The author mentions some puzzling questions about prayer. What questions about prayer puzzle you the most?
2. Howard Hendricks taught the author a great deal about prayer. Identify someone in your life who models effective praying. What do you admire most about this person's prayer life?
3. How would you respond to the question, "How can we differentiate

between those decisions that require prayer and those decisions that simply require action?" Do we need to seek God's direction for *every* decision? Why or why not?

4. If you didn't already do so while reading chapter 4, take time now to make a worry list and then transfer those items to your prayer list. Spend ten minutes praying over the items on your new prayer list.
5. Describe a time in your life when you experienced the supernatural peace of God.
6. Take a few moments, close your eyes, and ask God to speak to you right now. Do you sense His Spirit communicating any of His desires for your life, such as sins to be abandoned, relationships to be mended, or commands to be obeyed?
7. Why don't you pray more than you have been recently? Identify your greatest barrier to a more effective prayer life. What can you do *today* to remove that barrier?
8. Using the author's three ingredients for a successful prayer life (a period, a place, and a pad), formulate a simple plan for making prayer a priority in your life. Be specific. "Starting _____, I will set aside this time _____ to talk with and listen to God in this location _____ and to spend some time recording His insights to me ____ (in a tablet, in a notebook, on my computer)."

Chapter 5: Signs, Circumstances, and the Will of God

1. Have you ever asked God to give you a special sign that would clarify His will? Describe the outcome of your experience.
2. Why do you think the Bible (especially the Old Testament) contains so many accounts of supernatural revelations from God?
3. Can you cite an example from your own life in which a desire for a

sign from God was motivated by a lack of faith? Did you receive the sign you requested? If not, how did you respond?

4. Do you agree with the author's statement that if you're going to ask for a supernatural sign, it should be something really supernatural (like a letter from the president)? Why or why not?
5. Why do you think there is such a growing interest in supernatural signs and manifestations of God's Spirit? Do you think it's a positive or negative development? Why?
6. Picture a dilemma you are confronting right now. Is there any "natural" sign you could request that actually would be wisdom in disguise?
7. What is the greatest single mistake you see most Christians make regarding supernatural signs?
8. What one insight about supernatural signs has most impressed you from chapter 5? How will that insight affect the way you go about determining God's direction in your life?

Chapter 6: Who Speaks for God?

1. Before you read this chapter, did you consider other people as a primary channel through whom God speaks to you? Why or why not?
2. Identify the authority figures in your life. Which ones do you have the most difficulty submitting to? Why?
3. Do you believe that God can speak to you through non-Christian authority figures? Why or why not?
4. Do you agree with the author's explanation of submission as it relates to husbands and wives? Why or why not?
5. Identify a major decision you need to make in the next three months. What people could offer you wise counsel concerning this decision? Is there any reason—such as hidden agendas—that you should be cautious in following their counsel?

6. Do you agree with the author's view that an advisor's knowledge about a particular issue is more important than his or her spirituality? Why or why not?
7. Do you tend to listen to the advice of fellow church members? Why or why not?
8. Can you list several people in your life who love you enough to correct you? Do you believe they feel free to do so? Why or why not?

Chapter 7: To Thine Own Self Be True

1. When you're trying to discern God's direction in a specific situation, do you typically use your own desires as a way to find God's will? Why or why not?
2. What advice would you have offered to Mary Cleminson about her dream of becoming a motivational speaker? Why?
3. As you reflect on your life, can you remember a time when your personal desires were in line with God's desires? Have there been times when your desires conflicted with God's will? How do you explain the difference between those two situations?
4. Do you agree with the author that the task of transforming our desires (sanctification) is a cooperative process between God and us? Why or why not?
5. Set aside time this week to answer the questions Bobb Biehl poses under the heading Desires Put to the Test on page 131.
6. When should we use common sense as a guide to determining God's will? Is common sense ever irrelevant in seeking God's direction for our lives? If so, when?
7. Do you think you are spiritually healthy enough to trust the desires of your heart? If not, what do you need to change?
8. What's the most important insight you gained from chapter 7?

Chapter 8: Marriage, Money, and the Will of God

1. Do you agree that God has one specific person He intends to be your mate (if He desires for you to marry)? Why or why not?
2. If you're married, how did you determine God's will about the selection of a mate? If you're single, how can you know whether God intends for you to marry?
3. Is it ever permissible for a Christian to marry a non-Christian? Why do you think the command of 2 Corinthians 6:14 is so often violated today?
4. How would you rank the Five P's for selecting a mate (precepts, prayer, practicality, preference, and providence) in order of importance? If you're discussing this in a group, be ready to defend your answer.
5. Can you cite an instance in your life when the providence of God overrode your choice of a potential mate or career?
6. Do you agree or disagree with the author's claim that farmers and truck drivers are called by God to their work? Why?
7. Spend some time answering the three questions about your lifework found under the heading Preference: Do What You Want to Do on page 153.
8. Do you believe you're performing your lifework at this time? If not, why?

Chapter 9: God's Thundering Silence

1. Describe a period in your life when you questioned God's silence.
2. What does Jesus' experience on the cross teach us about God's silence? Is it right to express disappointment with God? Why or why not?
3. Do you agree with the author that God's silence is more often the rule than the exception? Why or why not?
4. How would you answer a friend who asked, "If I'm a Christian and God already has forgiven me, why should I confess my sins to Him?"

5. What fear is keeping you from hearing God's voice? If you knew for sure that the thing you fear never would become reality, what would you do differently in your life?
6. Can you cite an episode in which your timing was different from God's timing? What did you learn from the experience?
7. If we are to pray according to God's will, does that mean we can always know God's will? If not, how should we pray?
8. Does God's silence always strengthen our faith? Why or why not?

Chapter 10: The Shepherd's Safety Net

1. Explain your concept of the sovereignty of God.
2. Do you have difficulty accepting that God is in control of all that happens in His universe? Why or why not?
3. How would you answer someone who says, "Since God is good, it's impossible that His perfect plan could include evil"?
4. What's the difference between the sovereignty of God and fatalism?
5. Under the heading Our Responsibilities, the author explains that the sovereignty of God doesn't negate our responsibility for making wise choices, doesn't protect us from the consequences of disobedience, and doesn't guarantee an answer to all of our questions. In your opinion, which of these is the most common misunderstanding of God's sovereignty? Explain.
6. As you consider the three benefits of God's sovereignty—peace from the past, comfort for the present, and assurance for the future—which one is most important to you? Why?
7. Looking back on your life, has there been a time when you doubted God's sovereignty? Has that doubt been resolved? How?
8. What is the most helpful concept you've learned from reading this book? What is the single most important principle you could begin to apply today that would help you hear God's voice more clearly?

Americans' Views on Finding God's Will

A National Opinion Study

The following information is adapted from the reported findings of an opinion study commissioned by WaterBrook Press and conducted by Barna Research Group, Ltd., in October and November 2000. The research was conducted in OmniPoll.™ In a nationwide sample, 1,020 adults across the United States were asked seven questions focused on their perceptions of finding God's will.

Study Objectives

The researchers had the following objectives:

- To determine the percentage of American adults who are facing decisions for which they want direction from God.
- To determine how people discern God's will for their lives. Three models were tested: the rational approach, the experiential approach, and the formulaic approach.
- To determine what percentage of adults can recall one or more specific instances of God's speaking to them through unusual or supernatural means or circumstances.
- To determine adults' views on God's will regarding one of the most

important decisions any person makes: the choice of a marriage partner.

- To determine adults' views on God's sovereignty: specifically, whether God's ultimate plan for their lives can be thwarted by the mistakes they make.

The research found that Americans strongly favor one of the three methods of finding God's will. Overall, 3 out of 5 adults closely align themselves with the rational approach. The percentages among people of faith, with the exclusion of those who attend mainline churches, were even higher. Opinion was more evenly split on the other two tested approaches. The contention of the research sponsors is that while most people are eager to receive God's direction in their lives, they adhere to methods that present an incomplete picture of how God reveals His will to them. Contradictory teachings and beliefs regarding the "right" way to find God's will actually make it more difficult for people to accurately discern His plan for their lives.

Survey Methodology

The OmniPoll™ included 1,020 telephone interviews conducted among a representative sample of adults over the age of 18 within the 48 continental states. The survey was conducted in October and November of 2000. All interviews were conducted from the Barna Research Group telephone center in Ventura, California. The sampling error for OmniPoll is plus or minus three percentage points, at the 95% confidence level.

The survey calls were made at various times during the day and evening so that individuals selected for inclusion were contacted on different days, at different times of the day, to maximize the possibility of contact. This quality-control procedure ensures that individuals in the sampling frame have an equivalent probability of inclusion within the survey, thereby increasing the survey's reliability.

Based upon U.S. Census data sources, regional and ethnic quotas were designed to ensure that the final group of adults interviewed reflected the distribution of adults nationwide and adequately represented the three primary ethnic groups within the United States (those groups that comprise at least 10% of the population: white, black, and Hispanic). The final survey data were balanced according to gender.

In this study the cooperation rate among participants was 80%. This is an unusually high rate (the industry norm is about 60%), and it significantly raises the confidence we may place in the resulting statistics. In every survey there are a variety of ways in which the accuracy of the data may be affected. The cooperation rate is one such potential cause of error in measurement: The lower the cooperation rate, the less representative the respondents interviewed may be of the population from which they were drawn, thereby reducing the accuracy of the results. Other sources of error include question-design bias, question-order bias, interviewer mistakes, sampling error, and respondent deception. Many of these types of errors cannot be accurately estimated. However, having a high cooperation rate does enhance the reliability of the information procured.

The survey respondents were classified according to a number of "subgroups," including the following:

Gender—male or female

Age—in the ranges 18 to 34 years ("Busters"), 35 to 53 years ("Boomers"), 54 to 72 years ("Builders"), and 73 years and older ("Seniors")

Marital status—currently married, currently unmarried, currently divorced, or at one time divorced

Education level—high school or less, some college, or college graduate (including some who hold graduate degrees)

Annual household pretax income—less than $30,000; between $30,000 and $60,000; or $60,000 and higher

Region—Northeast, South, Midwest, or West

Ethnicity—white, black, or Hispanic

Religious identification—Respondents were classified in various faith groups either according to their answers to questions or based on the individual respondent's self-description. The faith subgroups are as follows:

Self-descriptions—Respondents identified themselves as Christian, atheist, or "other faith" (a religious faith other than Christian).

Denominations—Four major groupings were used: Catholic (those attending a Catholic church); Baptist (those attending a church in one of the Baptist denominations); mainline (those attending a church within one of the following denominations: Episcopal, Methodist, Lutheran, Presbyterian, or United Church of Christ); and Protestant non-mainline (those attending a church affiliated with a Protestant denomination other than those listed under the mainline category).

"Born-again"—This classification does *not* refer to people calling themselves by this label. Barna Research surveys include two questions regarding beliefs that are used to classify people as born-again or not born-again. To be classified as a born-again Christian, individuals must say that they have made a personal commitment to Jesus Christ that is still important in their life today and that after they die they will go to heaven because they have confessed their sins and accepted Jesus Christ as their Savior. People who meet these criteria are classified as born-again regardless of whether they would use that term to describe themselves.

"Evangelical"—This term is applied to born-again Christians (see previous explanation) who meet seven additional criteria: (1) saying their faith is very important in their life; (2) believing they have a responsibility to share their faith in Christ with non-Christians; (3) believing in the existence of Satan; (4) believing that eternal salvation is gained through God's grace alone, not through their efforts; (5) believing that Jesus Christ lived a sinless life while on earth; (6) believing the Bible is accurate in all that it

teaches; (7) choosing an orthodox definition of God. As defined in this survey report, the term "evangelical" has no relationship to a person's church attendance, church membership, or denominational affiliation.

Religious activities—Respondents were asked if, within the past week, they had been involved in one of these three activities: attending church, reading the Bible, or attending a meeting of a small group.

On the following pages is a summary of the responses to each of the seven questions commissioned by WaterBrook Press in this opinion study. Each question is presented verbatim, followed by the "overall response," which reflects the percentages for all respondents. Then an analysis provides commentary on the responses, followed by important findings and statistically significant patterns in the ways different subgroups answered each question.

Seeking God's Direction

Question

"You are currently facing a decision in your life for which you would like to get direction from God." Do you agree or disagree with that statement? Do you (agree/disagree) strongly or somewhat?

Overall Response

Agree strongly: 46%
Agree somewhat: 22%
Disagree somewhat: 15%
Disagree strongly: 14%
Don't know: 3%

Analysis

In spite of widespread disagreement surrounding the best way to find God's will, we know that Americans are eager to receive His guidance in their lives. Overall, the researchers found that more than two-thirds of all American adults (68%), and more than 8 out of 10 born-again adults (83%), agreed to some degree with the statement: "You are currently facing a decision in your life for which you would like to get direction from God." Nearly half of all adults (46%), regardless of their faith, *agreed strongly* with this statement.

The response to this statement underscores the hunger people have to at least factor in God's desires as they make decisions. The percentage of adults who strongly agreed with the statement, indicating a more ardent desire to receive God's direction, understandably was higher among practicing Christians. However, nearly 6 out of 10 (58%) of those who identified themselves as non-Christians agreed to some extent (strongly or somewhat) with the statement. It's significant that adults who don't practice the Christian faith still have a high regard for knowing the will of God in a decision they are facing.

A second important finding relates to the way the statement was worded: "You are *currently* facing a decision in your life for which you would like to get direction from God" [emphasis added]. The response to this statement does not signal a vague sense that receiving guidance from God might be a good idea. The respondents were agreeing that they had a specific, immediate need for God's direction in their lives. This says much about the depth of interest in knowing God's will.

Subgroup Patterns

Not surprisingly, those committed to the Christian faith are more likely than non-Christians to be seeking God's guidance. Compared to 58% of non-Christians, 83% of born-again Christians and 87% of evangelicals are looking to God for specific guidance. When the data are segmented by denominational groups, those who attend non-mainline churches are more likely than others to be seeking God's direction in their lives (80% agreed with the survey statement). As well, 3 out of 4 (75%) of those who attend a church affiliated with a charismatic denomination (Assemblies of God, Pentecostal/Foursquare, or Church of God) are seeking God's direction for a specific decision they are facing.

In addition to the differences among various faith-related groups, other segments of the population emerge as more likely to be seeking God's guidance. Specifically, blacks (85%) and southerners (78%) are more likely than others to agree that they are looking to God for counsel. As well, those with a lower household income ($30,000 or less a year) and those who have not attended college are more likely than others to be seeking God's direction (76% and 72%, respectively).

(Average: 46% of all adults *strongly agree* that they are currently faced with a decision for which they would like God's direction.)

Segments MOST likely to be seeking God's direction:

- evangelicals (76%)
- attenders of charismatic churches (75%)
- blacks (72%)
- those who attend a small group (70%)
- regular Bible readers (65%)
- born-again Christians (64%)
- those who attend a non-mainline church (61%)
- southerners (60%)
- church attenders (59%)
- those who earn less than $30,000 (53%)
- those who have a high school diploma or less (50%)

Segments LEAST likely to be seeking God's direction:

- atheists (10%)
- non-Christians (34%)
- those who earn at least $60,000 (34%)
- those who attend a mainline church (34%)
- westerners (35%)
- northeasterners (38%)
- college graduates (40%)

SUPERNATURAL ENCOUNTERS WITH GOD

Question

"You can recall a specific decision in your life when God revealed what you should do through some supernatural means such as a dream, a sign, a vision, a voice, or some other unusual or miraculous circumstance." Do you agree or disagree with that statement? Do you (agree/disagree) strongly or somewhat?

Overall Response

Agree strongly: 32%
Agree somewhat: 22%
Disagree somewhat: 19%
Disagree strongly: 24%
Don't know: 4%

Analysis

Those who follow trends in our culture say Americans have a renewed interest in spiritual things. This is said to be true even among adults who don't identify with the Christian faith or with any other formal religious system. The response to this question would seem to bear that out.

Slightly more than half of all adults, regardless of their faith orientation, agreed with the statement: "You can recall a specific decision in your life when God revealed what you should do through some supernatural means such as a dream, a sign, a vision, a voice, or some other unusual or miraculous circumstance." Nearly two-thirds of born-again Christians indicated they have had an encounter with God of the sort described in the statement.

It's significant to note the wording of the statement. The respondents were not simply agreeing that they had experienced some type of supernatural encounter with God. They indicated that God had given them specific direction through a dream, a vision, a sign or voice, or some other "unusual or miraculous circumstance." Indeed, 54% of all adults said they could recall such an occurrence. Nearly 1 in 3 (32%) agreed strongly and another 22% agreed somewhat. Note that one-fifth of all adults gave tentative support to the idea (agreed somewhat), perhaps suggesting that they're not sure the experience was truly supernatural. This finding is important in relation to a later question related to the experiential approach to finding God's will.

Subgroup Patterns

Among born-again Christians, 64% agreed that they have had a supernatural encounter with God—40% agreed strongly and another 24% agreed somewhat. While evangelicals are just as likely as are born-again Christians to recall a miraculous experience with God (62% of evangelicals agreed with the statement), evangelicals are more likely than others to be *certain* of the experience. In total, 51% of evangelicals agreed strongly with the statement, while only 11% offered soft support for such an experience. On the flip side, 26% of evangelicals are certain that they have *not* had a supernatural experience with God, which is significantly more than the 15% of born-again Christians who are sure they have not had this type of encounter.

Denominational differences emerge when looking at the self-report of these supernatural encounters. Nearly 7 in 10 (69%) of those who attend a charismatic church reported that they have had an unusual or supernatural experience with God. Similarly, 65% of Baptists and 64% of those who attend a non-mainline church agreed that they have had this type of experience. However, only 47% of Catholics reported the same. Interestingly, this number is consistent with findings among non-Christians.

Income and education also are related to an individual's report of an out-of-the-ordinary experience with God. Specifically, the affluent and college-educated are less likely to report such an experience (41% and 39%, respectively, agreed with the survey statement). Again, blacks (74%) are more likely than either whites or Hispanics to recall a supernatural encounter with God.

(Average: 32% of adults can recall a specific time when they felt God's leading through supernatural circumstances.)

Segments MOST likely to have had a supernatural encounter with God:

- evangelicals (51%)
- those who attend a small group (51%)
- blacks (47%)
- those who attend a charismatic church (46%)
- regular Bible readers (44%)
- those who attend a non-mainline church (42%)
- Baptists (42%)
- born-again Christians (40%)
- those who earn less than $30,000 (38%)
- southerners (37%)
- members of the baby-boom generation (37%)

Segments LEAST likely to have had a supernatural encounter with God:

- atheists (3%)
- those who earn at least $60,000 (23%)
- members of the "builder" generation (24%)
- college graduates (25%)
- non-Christians (26%)
- Catholics (26%)
- males (28%)

God's Role in Choosing Marriage Partners

Question

"You believe that if God intends a person to be married, God has only one specific marriage partner for them." Do you agree or disagree with that statement? Do you (agree/disagree) strongly or somewhat?

Overall Response

Agree strongly: 32%
Agree somewhat: 15%
Disagree somewhat: 21%
Disagree strongly: 25%
Don't know: 7%

Analysis

An ongoing debate within some Christian circles centers on God's will as it relates to the selection of a marriage partner. Could any one of a number of potential mates be God's choice, or does He have in mind two specific individuals that He wants to join in marriage? In other words, is there only one "right" person for you to marry, or is the choice of a spouse more a matter of finding the best match while taking into account the requirements of Scripture?

Overall, about 1 in 3 adults strongly agreed with the statement: "You believe that if God intends a person to be married, God has only one specific marriage partner for them." That means that 32% of all adults, including nearly 1 in 4 non-Christians, believe that in God's eyes there is only one right person for them to marry (assuming that He intends for that person to get married).

When it comes to God's role in selecting marriage partners, Americans' opinions are split down the middle. Just under half (47%) of all adults agree to some extent—and 46% disagree to some extent—that God has only one "right" mate in mind for each person. Of those who hold the strongest opinions, 32% strongly agree that God has in mind one "perfect" partner for every person who is destined for marriage, and 25% strongly disagree. Thus, about half lean one way or the other on the issue, but they aren't really that sure.

Subgroup Patterns

Taking a closer look at the data, subgroup patterns emerge among those who strongly accept this notion. Compared to 32% of adults in general who strongly contend that God narrows the choice down to only *one* potential mate, 44% of all born-again Christians and 52% of evangelicals believe that way. Baptists also are more likely than others to maintain that God does have a specific partner in mind for those He intends to be married (45% of Baptists strongly agree).

Once again, income, education, region, and ethnicity correspond to an individual's belief in this area. Blacks (42%), those with a lower annual income (38%), southerners (37%), and those with no college education (36%) are more likely than others to strongly contend that God does have a specific marriage partner in mind for each person.

(Average: 32% of adults believe that God has one specific marriage partner for everyone whom He intends to be married.)

Segments MOST likely to believe that God has in mind one specific marriage partner:

- evangelicals (52%)
- those who attend a small group (48%)
- Baptists (45%)
- born-again Christians (44%)
- regular Bible readers (43%)
- blacks (42%)
- those who earn less than $30,000 (38%)
- southerners (37%)
- those who have a high school diploma or less (36%)

Segments LEAST likely to believe that God has in mind one specific marriage partner:

- atheists (6%)
- those who earn at least $60,000 (23%)
- college graduates (23%)
- non-Christians (24%)
- those who have been divorced (25%)

Our Mistakes and God's Plan

Question

"Even if you make a wrong decision, you believe that God's ultimate plan for your life will still happen." Do you agree or disagree with that statement? Do you (agree/disagree) strongly or somewhat?

Overall Response

Agree strongly: 53%
Agree somewhat: 24%
Disagree somewhat: 9%
Disagree strongly: 9%
Don't know: 4%

Analysis

To what extent does God act, or choose to change His actions, in response to the behavior of humans? This is a discussion that touches on the free will we exercise versus God's sovereignty. Does God carry out His purposes in spite of us, or does He honor the choices we make—whether those choices are to our benefit or to our detriment?

This debate, and the related survey question, get at the issue of whether humans can derail God's plan through their mistakes and their failure to correctly discern His will. About half of all adults express a confidence in God's sovereignty, maintaining that His plan for their lives will ultimately come to pass regardless of the decisions they make. They don't believe that a failure to discern God's will is going to prevent God from working out His plan.

Among all adults, 53% strongly agreed with the survey statement: "Even if you make a wrong decision, you believe that God's ultimate plan for your life will still happen." Another 24% agreed somewhat that God will carry out His plan regardless of their actions. Conversely, nearly one-fifth (18%) of all adults disagreed to some extent that God's plans are unalterable.

Subgroup Patterns

Looking at those who are certain of God's sovereignty, it's not surprising that this belief is more widespread among Christians. Evangelicals are 33% more likely than all adults to completely agree that God's ultimate plan can't be sidetracked (71% strongly agreed with the survey statement). Similarly, Baptists (68%), those who attend a small group (66%), born-again Christians (66%), those who attend a charismatic church (66%), regular Bible readers (64%), and those who attend a non-mainline church (64%) are more likely than others to strongly believe that God's ultimate plans for them are unchangeable.

Women are more likely than men (57% to 49%, respectively) to have the mind-set that God's plans for their lives are unalterable. Again, blacks (69%), those in a lower income bracket (62%), southerners (58%), and those with no college education (57%) are more likely than others to strongly agree that God will carry out His will regardless of their own wrong decisions.

(Average: 53% of adults believe that God's ultimate plan will come to pass, regardless of the decisions they make.)

Segments MOST likely to believe that God's plan will always come to pass:

- evangelicals (71%)
- blacks (69%)
- Baptists (68%)

- born-again Christians (66%)
- those who attend a small group (66%)
- those who attend a charismatic church (66%)
- regular Bible readers (64%)
- those who attend a non-mainline church (64%)
- those who earn less than $30,000 (62%)
- southerners (58%)
- those who have a high school diploma or less (57%)
- females (57%)

Segments LEAST likely to believe that God's plan will always come to pass:

- atheists (20%)
- members of the "senior" generation (41%)
- non-Christians (45%)
- westerners (47%)
- college graduates (47%)
- males (49%)

Finding God's Will

The Three Approaches Studied

The survey examined which of three popular approaches to finding God's will adults prefer. Those three approaches, as defined by the author of this book, can be labeled "rational," "experiential," and "formulaic."

The rational approach refers to the belief that when a person is faced with a major decision, God wants that individual to make the best possible decision based on logically evaluating all of the options. The formulaic approach is the belief that when a person is faced with an important decision, God will indicate the best decision by causing certain things in the person's life (such as prayer, Bible reading, input from other people, and how the person personally feels) to all point in the same direction. The experiential approach is the belief that before a person makes an important decision, he should look for God to lead him to the best decision through the use of a sign, by speaking directly to the person, or by giving the individual some other supernatural indication of what to do.

To provide an accurate picture of those who most closely identify with each approach to finding God's will, the following analysis highlights the extreme positions only (strongly agree and strongly disagree).

The Rational Approach

Question

"You believe that when you make a major decision, God wants you to make the best possible decision based on logically evaluating all of the options." Do you agree or disagree with that statement? Do you (agree/disagree) strongly or somewhat?

Overall Response

Agree strongly: 59%
Agree somewhat: 24%
Disagree somewhat: 8%
Disagree strongly: 7%
Don't know: 3%

Analysis

Among the three methods studied, the rational approach was the method of choice for finding the will of God. Nearly 3 out of 5 adults (59%) strongly agreed with the statement: "You believe that when you make a major decision, God wants you to make the best possible decision based on logically evaluating all of the options."

This belief is consistent with a popular teaching that maintains that God gives us parameters, as set forth in the Bible, within which He wants us to live. But when we have to make a decision in an area for which there is no clear moral choice and no specific applicable scriptural teaching, God wants us to make the best choice after considering all the alternatives. This study proves the widespread appeal of this teaching.

It's significant that evangelical Christians were as likely as adults in general to agree with this approach to finding God's will. And overall, the rational approach was preferred to the second-most favored approach by 21%. The formulaic method was the second-place finisher in this study.

Subgroup Patterns

While nearly 7 in 10 (68%) of born-again Christians strongly agree with the rational approach, evangelicals are just as likely as adults nationwide to strongly agree with this way of thinking (coming in at 60%). On the flip side, 7% of all adults, as well as 7% of evangelicals and 3% of born-again Christians, strongly *disagree* with using the rational approach when seeking God's will regarding a decision they need to make.

The rational method is more widely supported by Baptists than the other denominational groups investigated. Specifically, 73% of Baptists agree strongly with using the rational approach, compared to 68% of those who attend a non-mainline church, 67% of those who attend a charismatic church, 60% of Catholics, and 57% of those who attend a mainline church.

(Average: 59% of adults believe that God wants them to make the best possible decision by logically evaluating all of the options.)

Segments MOST likely to use the rational approach:

- blacks (76%)
- Baptists (73%)
- southerners (69%)
- those who attend a non-mainline church (68%)
- born-again Christians (68%)
- those who attend a charismatic church (67%)
- regular Bible readers (66%)
- those who earn less than $30,000 (61%)

Segments LEAST likely to use the rational approach:

- atheists (16%)
- non-Christians (52%)
- westerners (53%)

THE FORMULAIC APPROACH

Question

"You believe that when you have to make an important decision, God will show you the best decision by causing everything in your life to point you in the same direction, such as your prayers, what you read in the Bible, what other people tell you, and how you personally feel." Do you agree or disagree with that statement? Do you (agree/disagree) strongly or somewhat?

Overall Response

Agree strongly: 38%
Agree somewhat: 28%
Disagree somewhat: 16%
Disagree strongly: 15%
Don't know: 3%

Analysis

The formulaic approach is the second-most popular approach to finding God's will, among the three methods studied. About two out of five adults (38%) strongly agreed with the statement: "You believe that when you have to make an important decision, God will show you the best decision by causing everything in your life to point you in the same direction, such as your prayers, what you read in the Bible, what other people tell you, and how you personally feel." This corresponds with a teaching on God's will that maintains that God leads us by aligning certain prime indicators, such as answers to prayer, His leading through the Scriptures, the counsel of trusted Christians, circumstances in our lives, and our own personal feelings—often described as "having peace" about a certain decision or course of action.

Although the formulaic method ranked second behind the rational approach, it earned the allegiance of less than half of all adults. Meanwhile, 15% of all adults strongly *disagreed* with the formulaic approach.

Subgroup Patterns

Not surprisingly, support for the formulaic approach is more common among Christians than among adults in general. In total, 60% of evangelicals and 54% of born-again Christians likely follow some sort of "formula" when seeking God's will. The list of indicators might vary from person to person, but those who adhere to the formulaic approach would seek agreement among all the indicators. As a point of comparison, 5% of born-again Christians and 4% of evangelicals strongly *disagree* with this approach.

Within the camp of self-identified believers, there are some denominational differences. Specifically, charismatic churchgoers (63%) and Baptists (52%)—as well as those who attend a non-mainline church (53%)—are more likely than Catholics (30%) to use the formulaic approach when faced with a tough decision.

When it comes to gender differences, women are more likely than men to adopt the formulaic approach. Specifically, 44% of females, compared to 32% of males, look for agreement among these spiritual indicators to reveal God's plan for their lives.

(Average: 38% of adults believe that when faced with a decision, God will cause different areas of their life to agree and point them in the correct direction.)

Segments MOST likely to use the formulaic approach:

- those who attend a charismatic church (63%)
- blacks (61%)
- evangelicals (60%)
- those who attend a small group (60%)
- regular Bible readers (56%)
- born-again Christians (54%)
- those who attend a non-mainline church (53%)
- Baptists (52%)
- those who earn less than $30,000 (52%)
- southerners (50%)
- females (44%)
- those who have a high school diploma or less (43%)

Segments LEAST likely to use the formulaic approach:

- atheists (10%)
- those who earn at least $60,000 (26%)
- non-Christians (27%)
- college graduates (29%)
- Catholics (30%)
- westerners (30%)
- northeasterners (31%)
- males (32%)

THE EXPERIENTIAL APPROACH

Question

"You believe that before you make an important decision, you should look for God to lead you to the best decision by giving you a sign, by speaking directly to you, or by giving you some other supernatural indication of what to do." Do you agree or disagree with that statement? Do you (agree/disagree) strongly or somewhat?

Overall Response

Agree strongly: 27%
Agree somewhat: 21%
Disagree somewhat: 22%
Disagree strongly: 27%
Don't know: 3%

Analysis

The experiential approach was the least favored of the three methods studied. When faced with a decision, about one-quarter (27%) of all adults (and 38% of born-again Christians) opt for the experiential approach. Unlike the other two methods, Americans are just as likely to strongly support this approach as to not support it. An equal number—27%—both strongly agreed and strongly disagreed with the survey statement: "You believe that before you make an important decision, you should look for God to lead you to the best decision by giving you a sign, by speaking directly to you, or by giving you some other supernatural indication of what to do."

This method fits the teaching that God reveals His will by "speaking directly to us" through a dream, a vision, a miraculous sign, or some other out-of-the-ordinary means. This method clearly lags in popularity. Among all adults, it ran 11 points behind the formulaic method and 32 points behind the top-ranked rational approach.

Subgroup Patterns

As one might expect, committed Christians are more likely than others to seek God's leading through miraculous circumstances. Nearly half (47%) of evangelicals and 38% of born-again Christians strongly agreed that they seek supernatural leading from God when faced with a decision. Conversely, 18% of born-again Christians and 21% of evangelicals strongly *disagreed* with this approach.

When it comes to different denominations, specific groups of churchgoers are more apt to look for supernatural leading from God than are others. Compared to 40% of those who attend a non-mainline church (as well as 38% of Baptists and 35% of charismatic churchgoers) who strongly agree that they look for supernatural signs from God, only half as many

Catholics and mainline church attenders hold the same belief. Only 1 in 5 (20%) of both Catholics and those who attend a mainline church strongly agreed with the experiential approach.

(Average: 27% of adults believe that they should look for a supernatural leading from God when faced with a decision.)

Segments MOST likely to use the experiential approach:

- those who attend a small group (52%)
- blacks (52%)
- evangelicals (47%)
- regular Bible readers (40%)
- those who attend a non-mainline church (40%)
- born-again Christians (38%)
- Baptists (38%)
- those who attend a charismatic church (35%)
- southerners (33%)
- those who earn less than $30,000 (33%)
- those who have a high school diploma or less (32%)

Segments LEAST likely to use the experiential approach:

- atheists (6%)
- college graduates (17%)
- non-Christians (20%)
- those who attend a mainline church (20%)
- Catholics (20%)
- those who earn at least $60,000 (20%)
- whites (22%)

Who Uses Which Approach?

Within the Christian community, definite preferences appear among the three methods studied. While Christians are more likely than the average adult to agree with any one of these three methods of finding God's will, the approaches rank differently within various segments of the Christian community. Looking at different segments of the Christian population—born-again Christians, evangelicals, Baptists, Catholics, and so on—shows unique patterns.

The following bullet points highlight interesting conclusions across various population segments related to the rational, experiential, and formulaic approaches to finding God's will.

- While the rational method is the most commonly used approach among all adults (and even among born-again Christians), evangelicals are just as likely to agree with the rational approach as they are to agree with the formulaic strategy. Both methods are backed by 60% of evangelicals.
- Born-again Christians are 75% more likely to align themselves with the rational method than they are to agree with the experiential approach (68% to 38%, respectively).
- Overall, Catholics, those who attend a mainline church, and non-Christians are similar in their support of the experiential method—only 20% of adults in each of these groups strongly agree that they look for supernatural signs to determine God's will.
- While blacks are more likely than whites to agree with any of the three approaches, the largest gap in opinions between these two groups relates to the experiential approach. Blacks are 135% more likely than are whites to agree with the experiential approach, 79% more likely to agree with the formulaic approach, and 35% more likely to agree with the rational approach.

No Method Corners the Market

There is no one method that has earned the allegiance of all Christians, and few Christian segments align themselves closely with any one of these three methods of determining God's will.

Analyzing the data slightly differently, a clearer picture emerges related to the popularity of each approach among the different groups. Support for each approach was categorized in the following categories: widespread (at least 65% of the population strongly agreed with the approach); common (50% to 64% strongly agreed); occasional (30% to 49%); and sporadic (less than 30%). The following bullet points highlight some interesting conclusions.

- The rational approach is the only method of finding God's will that has widespread acceptance among any of the segments investigated—which were Baptist, those who attend a non-mainline church, charismatic churchgoers, born-again Christians, southerners, and blacks.
- Among evangelicals, no single approach received widespread support, but both the rational and the formulaic methods emerged as common (50% to 64% strongly agreed).
- Except among blacks, looking for supernatural leading from God emerged as an occasional, and oftentimes sporadic, means of seeking the will of God.
- Among non-Christians (who make up nearly 60% of U.S. adults), the rational approach registers as a common belief, while relatively small proportions of this group hold the other two viewpoints.

Who's Unclear on Finding God's Will?

A large number of adults aren't clear on how they obtain God's guidance when they are faced with big decisions. Although many Americans registered an opinion, how they deal with major life choices is still uncertain. Here is the evidence.

- For each of the three approaches studied, at least one-third of all respondents offered a soft response—"sitting on the fence" with a somewhat agree or somewhat disagree position (or opting for a "don't know" response).
- Few adults strongly opposed any of the three approaches. The experiential method drew the strongest opposition (27% strongly disagreed), while only 15% challenged the formulaic approach, and 7% argued against the rational approach.
- While one-third of all adults (32%) agreed strongly with one of the three approaches, another 38% registered their support for more than one approach. Just over 1 in 5 (21%) strongly agreed with two of the three approaches, and 17% strongly agreed with all three. This overlap in support demonstrates the duality in many adults' thinking about the best way to discern God's leading when faced with a major decision.
- A noticeable segment of adults did not align with any one of the three approaches. In total, 3 out of 10 did not strongly support any of the methods for finding God's will.

NOTES

Chapter 1

1. Haddon W. Robinson, *Decision Making by the Book* (Grand Rapids, Mich.: Discovery House, 1998), 9. Used by permission of Discovery House Publishers, Box 3566, Grand Rapids, Michigan 49501. All rights reserved.
2. Robinson, *Decision Making by the Book*, 11.
3. M. Blaine Smith, *Knowing God's Will* (Downers Grove, Ill.: InterVarsity, 1991), 58. Used with permission from InterVarsity Press, P.O. Box 1400, Downers Grove, IL 60515.

Chapter 2

1. George Muller, as quoted in David Jeremiah, *Prayer: The Great Adventure* (Sisters, Oreg.: Multnomah, 1997), 113-4.
2. Charles R. Swindoll, *Moses* (Nashville, Tenn.: Word, 1999), 274.
3. C. S. Lewis, as quoted in Bruce Waltke, *Finding the Will of God* (Gresham, Oreg.: Vision House, 1995), 6.

Chapter 3

1. Bruce Waltke, *Finding the Will of God* (Gresham, Oreg.: Vision House, 1995), 90.
2. Erwin W. Lutzer, *Seven Reasons Why You Can Trust the Bible* (Chicago: Moody, 1998), 73, 74-5.
3. Haddon W. Robinson, *Decision Making by the Book* (Grand Rapids, Mich.: Discovery House, 1998), 19. Used by permission of Discovery House Publishers, Box 3566, Grand Rapids, Michigan 49501. All rights reserved.

4. Paul Little, *Affirming the Will of God* (Downers Grove, Ill.: InterVarsity, 1971), 28-9, quoted in M. Blaine Smith, *Knowing God's Will* (Downers Grove, Ill.: InterVarsity, 1991), 28-9. Used with permission from InterVarsity Press, P.O. Box 1400, Downers Grove, IL 60515.
5. As quoted in Charles R. Swindoll, *The Mystery of God's Will* (Nashville, Tenn.: Word, 1999), 23-4.
6. John Ortberg, *The Life You've Always Wanted* (Grand Rapids, Mich.: Zondervan, 1997), 146.
7. John MacArthur Jr., *Found: God's Will* (Colorado Springs, Colo.: Chariot Victor, 1973), 28-9.
8. Swindoll, *The Mystery of God's Will,* 44-5.
9. Oswald Chambers, as quoted in Steve Farrar, *Standing Tall* (Sisters, Oreg.: Multnomah, 1994), 177.

Chapter 4

1. As quoted in Max Lucado, *Just Like Jesus* (Nashville, Tenn.: Word, 1998), 71.
2. Eugene Peterson, *Reversed Thunder* (San Francisco: Harper & Row, 1988), 93, quoted in Chap Clark, *The Performance Illusion* (Colorado Springs, Colo.: NavPress, 1993), 123.
3. Henry T. Blackaby and Claude V. King, *Experiencing God* (Nashville, Tenn.: Broadman & Holman, 1994), 109.
4. C. S. Lewis, *The Efficacy of Prayer in the World Last Night and Other Essays* (New York: Harcourt, Brace & World, 1959), 9, and C. S. Lewis, *Work and Prayer in God in the Dock* (Grand Rapids, Mich.: Eerdmans, 1970), 104-7, quoted in M. Blaine Smith, *Knowing God's Will* (Downers Grove, Ill.: InterVarsity, 1991), 89. Used with permission from InterVarsity Press, P.O. Box 1400, Downers Grove, IL 60515.
5. Bill Hybels, "Why We Shouldn't Give Up on Prayer" (Carol Stream, Ill.: *Preaching Today,* 1998), audiotape no. 184.

6. Jim Cymbala, *Fresh Wind, Fresh Fire* (Grand Rapids, Mich.: Zondervan, 1997), 57.
7. Paul Little, *Affirming the Will of God* (Downers Grove, Ill.: InterVarsity, 1971), 17-18, quoted in Smith, *Knowing God's Will*, 91. Used with permission from InterVarsity Press, P.O. Box 1400, Downers Grove, IL 60515.
8. Gordon MacDonald, *Ordering Your Private World* (Nashville, Tenn.: Oliver-Nelson, 1984), 160.
9. Author's files.
10. Ron Mehl, *The Ten(der) Commandments* (Sisters, Oreg.: Multnomah, 1998), 47-8.
11. John Piper, *Desiring God: Tenth Anniversary Expanded Edition* (Sisters, Oreg.: Multnomah, 1996), 182, quoted in David Jeremiah, *Prayer: The Great Adventure* (Sisters, Oreg.: Multnomah, 1997), 45-6.
12. Luci Shaw, *Life Path: Personal and Spiritual Growth Through Journal Writing* (Portland, Oreg.: Multnomah, 1991), 34, quoted in Jeremiah, *Prayer: The Great Adventure*, 240.

Chapter 5

1. Bruce Waltke, *Finding the Will of God* (Gresham, Oreg.: Vision House, 1995), 38.
2. Waltke, *Finding the Will of God*, 48-56.
3. Haddon W. Robinson, *Decision Making by the Book* (Grand Rapids, Mich.: Discovery House, 1998), 29-30. Used by permission of Discovery House Publishers, Box 3566, Grand Rapids, Michigan 49501. All rights reserved.
4. Garry Friesen, *Decision Making and the Will of God* (Portland, Oreg.: Multnomah, 1980), 224-5.

Chapter 6

1. Vance Havner, *It Is Toward Evening* (Westwood, N.J.: Revell, 1968), 39-40, quoted in Charles R. Swindoll, *Esther: A Woman of Strength & Dignity* (Nashville, Tenn.: Word, 1997), 177-8.
2. Haddon W. Robinson, *Decision Making by the Book* (Grand Rapids, Mich.: Discovery House, 1998), 112. Used by permission of Discovery House Publishers, Box 3566, Grand Rapids, Michigan 49501. All rights reserved.
3. Henry T. Blackaby and Claude V. King, *Experiencing God* (Nashville, Tenn.: Broadman & Holman, 1994), 129.
4. Bruce Waltke, *Finding the Will of God* (Gresham, Oreg.: Vision House, 1995), 120.

Chapter 7

1. F. B. Meyer, *Devotional Commentary on Philippians* (Grand Rapids, Mich.: Kregel, 1979), 10, quoted in David Jeremiah, *Turning Toward Joy* (Wheaton, Ill.: Victor, 1992), 86.
2. Bobb Biehl, *Asking to Win* (Lake Mary, Fla.: Masterplanning Group International, 1996), 9, 18.
3. Bruce Waltke, *Finding the Will of God* (Gresham, Oreg.: Vision House, 1995), 100.

Chapter 9

1. Author's files.
2. Edmund Morris, *Dutch* (New York: Random House, 1999), 592.
3. Morton Kelsey, *The Other Side of Silence* (New York: Paulist, 1976), 105, quoted in Peter Lord, *Hearing God* (Grand Rapids, Mich.: Baker, 1988), 76.
4. Ben Patterson, quoted in John Ortberg, "Waiting on God" (Carol Stream, Ill.: Preaching Today) transcript of audiotape no. 199, 2.

5. Sören Kierkegaard, *Philosophical Fragments*, trans. David Swenson (Princeton, N.J.: Princeton University Press, 1962), quoted in Philip Yancey, *Disappointment with God* (Grand Rapids, Mich.: Zondervan, 1988), 208.
6. Henri Nouwen, quoted in Ortberg, "Waiting on God," 3.
7. V. Raymond Edman, *In Quietness and Confidence* (Colorado Springs, Colo.: Scripture Press, 1953), 63, quoted in Charles R. Swindoll, *Moses* (Nashville, Tenn.: Word, 1999), 88.

Chapter 10

1. W. A. Criswell, *Ephesians* (Grand Rapids, Mich.: Zondervan, 1974), 28-9.
2. Eugene Peterson, *Run with the Horses: The Quest for Life at Its Best* (Downers Grove, Ill.: InterVarsity, 1983), quoted in Charles R. Swindoll, *The Mystery of God's Will* (Nashville, Tenn.: Word, 1999), 101.
3. Charles R. Swindoll, *David* (Dallas: Word, 1997), 15.
4. A. W. Tozer, *The Tozer Topical Reader*, compiled by Ron Eggert, 2 vols. (Camp Hill, Pa.: Christian Publications, 1998), 1:238.
5. Tozer, *The Tozer Topical Reader*, 1:239.

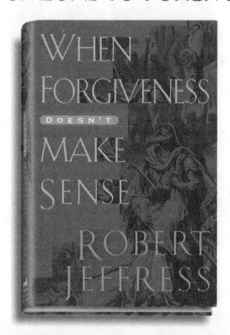